South Boo

NANCY MITFORD AND FRIENDS

Glenys Harrison grew up in Cumbria and was educated at Wyndham School and Aberystwyth University, where she read Russian. She lives in Cheltenham and was for many years the qualifications' specialist at the Universities and Colleges Admissions Service (UCAS). She is the sister of the artist and photographer Gareth Harrison.

Miss Harrison's other published works include *Homage to Robert Byron, Eton Society of Arts, Gertrude Lawrence,* and *Sir John T Davies : PPS to Lloyd George.*

Nancy Mitford and Friends

Glenys Harrison

South Books

Published in 2021 by South Books, 10 Southfield Manor Park, Cheltenham, GL53 9DJ, England

Second edition

Printed by Kindle Direct Publishing, an Amazon.com company

All rights reserved. No part of this book may be used or reproduced in any manner whatsoever without written permission except in the case of brief quotations used in critical articles and reviews.

ISBN : 9798504183268

For Mrs Barton, who encouraged me to go to university as well as writing a book

Contents

	Introduction	ix
1	Nancy Mitford	1
2	Mark Ogilvie-Grant	9
3	James Lees-Milne	33
4	Peter Watson	51
5	Evelyn Waugh	69
6	Robert Byron	93
7	Harold Acton	107
8	Lord Berners	117
	Who's Who	123
	Bibliography	127
	Index	141

INTRODUCTION

If you enjoy witty repartee and have a dry sense of humour you will feel at home in the world of Nancy Mitford and her friends. Much has been written about Miss Mitford and the world of the Bright Young Things over the years; the aim of this slim volume is not to duplicate what has already been said but rather to give readers a flavour of that world and make them want to delve more deeply into it for themselves. Nancy Mitford had many friends to whom she was close at different stages in her life, and I have tried to select a representative sample of them while at the same time concentrating on those who actually achieved something in life. As far as Nancy herself is concerned, a good way to gain an understanding of her world and appreciate the way her mind works is to read her letters to her friends and family. If you find her merely frivolous, bear in mind that women of her age and class were not expected to have an education or a career; they stayed quietly at home until they made a suitable marriage. Nancy's semi-autobiographical novel *The Pursuit of Love* captures what it was like to be a bored teenager growing up in a country house, and her early novels give us a snapshot of her time spent at country house parties.

Three friends who first helped to relieve the tedium of Nancy's life were Mark Ogilvie-Grant, James Lees-Milne, and Peter Watson. Mark Ogilvie-Grant was the cousin of Nancy's friend Nina Seafield, and she partied with them both in London and at country houses. After Mark moved abroad he and Nancy kept up a regular correspondence for the rest of his life. Not much has been written about Mark himself, though he sometimes pops up in biographies of various friends. I have included here everything that I was able to find out about him.

James-Lees Milne (known as Jim) was three years below Mark at Eton and Oxford, though they mixed in the same circles. He was a school friend of Nancy's brother Tom and used to visit the

Mitford family home during the school holidays. Jim has been described as 'The man who saved England' and the twelve published volumes of his diaries provide a good insight into his work for the National Trust in preserving country houses for the nation. His autobiography *Another Self* gives us some idea of what his early life was like, though the incidents he describes have been exaggerated for literary effect.

A third person who knew Nancy from when she was a young woman was Peter Watson, a wealthy patron of the arts. When I first began the research for this book there was not much open source material available about Peter, and I am grateful to Adrian Clark for giving me permission to use material from his recently-published book, *Queer Saint*. Peter was instrumental in furthering the careers of Francis Bacon and Lucian Freud among others.

A trio of friends from Oxford University - Evelyn Waugh, Robert Byron and Harold Acton - were also close to Nancy. Nancy met the novelist Evelyn Waugh when she was a friend of his first wife in the 1920s. After the break up of that marriage Nancy and Evelyn became firm friends, and Evelyn was her mentor and correspondent for the rest of his life. The published correspondence between them is a good showcase for their shared sense of humour. Evelyn's early novels, parodies of the lives of the Bright Young Things, have some brilliant flashes of wit, but the later volumes A *Handful of Dust* and *Scoop* are more considered and show him at his best. His more serious magnum opus, *Brideshead Revisited*, has stood the test of time and portrays the struggle with Catholic guilt.

Evelyn's friend Robert Byron wanted to familiarise himself with the major civilisations of the world by the time he was 30, and his journeys in Europe and Asia produced four travel books with learned descriptions of the art and architecture he saw. His idiosyncratic sense of humour shines through in the wonderful dialogues he has with some of the people he encounters on his journeys. Once you have adjusted to the flowery prose which Robert uses in order to avoid clichés you will be able to appreciate his work to the full. Nancy first met Robert at the parties of the Bright Young Things, and they became very close. After his untimely death she described him as the man she would have liked to marry, and added that it is the people with whom you shared jokes that you miss the most.

Harold Acton was a friend of Robert's at Eton and Oxford, but although he had heard a lot about Nancy he did not actually meet her until 1928. They probably met at a party. After World War Two, when Nancy was living in Paris and Harold was living in Florence, they corresponded until Nancy's death in 1973 and met up occasionally in Paris, Florence and Venice. The two volumes of Harold's memoirs are well written and give us a good insight into the society in which he moved, though he tells us virtually nothing about his private life.

Last but not least comes Gerald Berners, who was a neighbour of the Mitford family and somewhat older than Nancy and her other friends. Gerald and Nancy shared a bond because they had the same sense of humour. Nancy captures the essence of Gerald beautifully in *The Pursuit of Love*, where he is portrayed as the eccentric Lord Merlin who shares many of Gerald's characteristics.

Throughout the book I have used a selection of anecdotes to try and give a flavour of the lives of the friends, and I am grateful to my brother for pointing out that my previous books were rather factual. I hope you find this current volume more readable.

Glenys Harrison
Cheltenham
February 2016

CHAPTER ONE – NANCY MITFORD

Nancy Mitford (1904-1973) was an author, bon viveur, and the eldest of the six famous Mitford sisters.

* * * * *

Nancy Freeman-Mitford (known as Nancy Mitford) was born in London on 28th November 1904. She was the eldest daughter of the Honourable David Freeman-Mitford and his wife Sydney Bowles. David was the second son of Bertie Mitford, who had inherited Batsford House in Oxfordshire, as well as a lot of money and considerable estates, from a cousin. The Mitfords were related by marriage to several prominent British families including the Churchills, the Ogilvys, the Stanleys and the Russells. Nancy was the eldest of seven children, the others being Pamela, Tom, Diana, Unity, Jessica and Deborah.

Nancy's early childhood was spent in London where her father worked as business manager of *The Lady* magazine, a job provided for him by the proprietor, his father-in-law. Nancy's mother, Sydney, thought that children shouldn't be told off or shouted at, and made sure that Nancy's nanny and nursemaid went along with this. As a result the infant Nancy was self-centred and rather wild until Sydney decided to put a stop to the experimental upbringing and resort to more conventional methods. For a few months in 1910 Nancy attended the Francis Holland day school, but after that she and her sisters were educated at home by a succession of governesses.

When war broke out in 1914 Nancy's father, David, rejoined his old regiment and was sent to France. In May 1915 David's elder brother, Clement, was killed in action, then his father Bertie died in 1916. This made David the 2nd Baron Redesdale and owner of Batsford Park. Sydney promptly moved herself and the children into the extensive Batsford House, where the children had the run of the house and grounds. Their life at Batsford House and later at Asthall Manor is delightfully documented in Nancy's two semi-autobiographical novels, *The Pursuit of Love* (published in 1945) and *Love in a Cold Climate* (published in 1949). The library at Batsford was very well stocked and Nancy spent most of her time there reading. She developed a taste for biography, memoirs and letters, and liked Carlyle and Macaulay the best. She was the only sister who read. She shared her sisters' jokes and games, but longed to have someone with whom to discuss the books she read.

By 1919 David, now Lord Redesdale, had decided that Batsford House was too expensive to maintain. He sold the the house and the family moved to the smaller Asthall Manor, also in Oxfordshire, which was much more economical to run. Much to Nancy's regret, most of the books from the library at Batsford House were sold off. Then in 1926 the family moved to a Georgian farmhouse near the village of Swinbrook, a house which Lord Redesdale had had extensively remodelled.

When Nancy was 16 she was sent away to board for a year at Hatherop Castle, which was essentially a finishing school. There she made some life-long friends including Mary Milnes-Gaskell. In 1922 she went on a school trip which was to be the beginning of her life-long love affair with France and Italy. The visit included stays in Paris, Florence, Venice and Pisa, and established in Nancy a liking for the good things in life. She wrote home in wonder about the joys of having hot and cold running water in the hotel bedrooms, which was so different from her Spartan home life. She enjoyed eating out and browsing in clothes shops, but combined these excursions with intellectual pursuits such as visiting art galleries and churches. Visits to The Louvre in Paris and The Uffizi in

Florence reinforced her love of painting and made her long to see all the London art galleries. Nancy loved the architecture of Pisa and Venice and in later years she often visited Venice from her home in Paris. In Florence she daringly purchased a long necklace of coral beads, defying the taste of her class and time for conventional jewellery.

* * * * *

In November 1922 Nancy turned 18 and had a conventional coming-out ball at Asthall Manor. The following June she was presented at court. Once officially 'out' she could attend the balls and parties of the London Season (her parents rented a house in London for a few months each summer before buying a large house in Rutland Gate, Knightsbridge) and she devoted most of the next few years to socialising. As well as attending the traditional events of The Season, Nancy mixed with the Bright Young Things and frequented their cocktail parties and fancy dress balls in London. She became acquainted with various Oxford undergraduates, some of whom were contemporaries of her brother Tom and others of whom were of a slightly older generation. They included such people as Robert Byron, Hamish Erskine, Patrick Balfour, Henry Weymouth, Brian Howard, Michael Rosse, Peter Watson and James Lees-Milne. When Nancy and Tom were considered by their parents to be grown up they were allowed to have friends to stay at the family home in Oxfordshire at weekends, a situation of which they took full advantage. Sometimes Nancy and Mary Milnes-Gaskell sneaked off to Oxford to visit the undergraduates on their home territory, often without the knowledge or permission of their parents. One of Nancy's new débutante friends was the heiress Nina Seafield, and on several occasions Nancy and various friends attended house parties at Nina's two homes in Scotland,

Cullen Castle and Castle Grant. For one brief term Nancy managed to persuade her father to let her attend The Slade School of Art, but she left when she realised that she had little talent.

In the Autumn of 1928 Bryan Guinness, who was dating Nancy's sister Diana, was invited to stay at Swinbrook for a week and Nancy took the bold step of inviting Robert Byron to stay at the same time. She had met Robert at country house parties and got on extremely well with him as they shared the same sense of humour. She considered Robert to be an eligible young man (she only found out much later that he was gay) and was eager to spend more time with him. Robert and Bryan knew each other well; they had been friends ever since their Eton days. Their visit was a great success, and not long afterwards Bryan and Diana became engaged. Writing to his friend Michael Rosse about his visit, Robert said that he hadn't laughed so much for ages. Nancy wrote to her brother Tom about how much she had enjoyed the week, and said that she and Tom had been invited to go riding in Spain with Robert the following Easter. But at Easter Robert went off on his travels to India and Tibet, and in the meantime Nancy took up with Hamish Erskine.

Hamish St Clair-Erskine was the second son of the Earl of Rosslyn, and four years younger than Nancy. He was flamboyant, very good looking, charming, mischievous, silly, and a spendthrift. He also drank heavily and was a gambler. Hamish's father, also a gambler, was said to be the original 'Man Who Broke The Bank at Monte Carlo'. Unfortunately for Hamish his time at Eton had coincided with Tallulah Bankhead's time in the UK. Tallulah was a friend of Freda Dudley Ward, who was a friend of Hamish's mother, and she had introduced Hamish to the world of theatres, night clubs and heavy drinking while he was still a schoolboy. Nancy fell for the charming Hamish in a big way. Hamish was vain and liked to be admired. Nancy knew that he was selfish and irresponsible but thought she would be able to reform him, no doubt imaging that the love of a good woman would cure his drinking and gambling. Perhaps she also thought that Hamish would grow out of his homosexuality.

Nancy loved dressing Hamish up for fancy dress parties in both London and Scotland, sometimes even doing his hair with curling tongs. Hamish and Nancy often stayed with Nina Seafield at her homes in Scotland, where other frequent guests included Oliver Messel, Robert Byron, and Mark Ogilvie-Grant. Oliver loved to mimic White Russian refugee princesses, governesses and débutantes, Robert Byron had a fund of practical jokes, and Mark Ogilvie-Grant had a huge repertoire of Victorian ballads. Almost without realising it, Nancy frittered away several years of her life on Hamish. He appealed to her maternal instincts, but he was not husband material. Nancy's friend Harold Acton reckoned that Hamish prolonged Nancy's adolescence.

Nancy and Hamish had a long on-off relationship, though it seems as though Hamish never had any intention of marrying Nancy. Eventually Hamish had had enough, and in June 1933 he announced that he was going to marry the daughter of a London banker. He had no intention of marrying, but wanted an excuse to end his relationship with Nancy.

* * * * *

But Nancy had not been completely idle during her years with Hamish. In 1929 she had met and become friends with the author Evelyn Waugh, who encouraged her to write. Nancy's sister Diana had married Bryan Guinness in January of that year, and Nancy often went to stay with them in their London house. She had become close friends with two aspiring writers who shared a flat, Pansy Pakenham and Evelyn Gardner.

When Pansy married Henry Lamb Evelyn was worried that she would have to go back and live with her mother, and in a moment of apparent rashness she agreed to marry Evelyn Waugh. By the summer of 1929 He-Evelyn was away working on his second novel, *Vile Bodies*, and only spending weekends with his wife. It was arranged that Nancy would stay in the Evelyns' flat to keep She-Evelyn company during the week. Nancy and She-Evelyn entertained a lot, and one of their frequent guests was John Heygate. When She-Evelyn eloped with Heygate Nancy had to leave the flat, but she became a life-long friend of Evelyn Waugh.

Evelyn encouraged Nancy to write, and she was keen to supplement the small dress allowance she received from her parents. She wrote articles for *Vogue* and the *Tatler* on topical subjects, and her old friend Mark Ogilvie-Grant illustrated them. Then in 1930 she was commissioned to write a regular column for *The Lady*. Nancy's first novel, *Highland Fling*, was written during the winter of 1930-31, sitting over the drawing room fire at Swinbrook. The novel is a parody of the life of Nancy and her friends and family at that time, and juxtaposes the lives of the Bright Young Things and the traditional Scottish gentry. Albert Memorial Gates, who is based mainly on Robert Byron, collects Victoriana and enjoys playing practical jokes (Bertie was Nancy's pet name for Robert), while the character of Jane is based on Nancy herself. Nancy's father and various aunts and uncles are also parodied in the book, which was illustrated by Mark Ogilvie-Grant. Nancy wrote *Highland Fling*, which was published in March 1931, so that she would have some money on which she and Hamish could marry.

Immediately after the publication of *Highland Fling* Nancy began work on her second novel, *Christmas Pudding*. This second work is also set in a country house and once again looks at the differences between the Bright Young Things and the older generation. Paul Fotheringay, who is poor but charming, is based partially on John Betjeman but also has many attributes of Robert Byron. He is writing the biography of a female Victorian poet (a task which Betjeman aspired to) and has already written a book on the Byzantine Empire (Byron's book *The Byzantine Achievement* had been published in 1929). At one stage Paul has an amusing dream and the thing he remembers most about it is that he travelled first class on the train (Byron never had any money and usually travelled third class). Bobby Bobbin, who is being tutored by Paul, is partially based on Hamish during his time at Eton. He loves showing off and watching people's reactions. Nancy dedicated the book to Robert Byron (a fact which is sadly no longer mentioned in modern editions of the novel) and in the Autumn of 1932 she invited him to the book launch in London.

* * * * *

After the announcement of Hamish's engagement in June 1933 Nancy was in despair and bitterly unhappy, but after a few weeks she managed to pull herself together. In July she became engaged to Peter Rodd, whom she had met several times at parties. No doubt he was good company when he had been drinking, but Nancy and her family and friends soon found out what a crashing bore he was. Prod, as he was often known, was a younger son of the diplomat Sir Rennell Rodd who had been ambassador to Rome amongst other appointments. After he left Rome the Italian government gave the Rodds a piece of land at Posilipo, which was on a cliff overlooking the Bay of Naples, and they built a villa there. They also had a large and elegant apartment in Rome. Prod, who was clever but boring, was the model for Basil Seal in Evelyn Waugh's novels *Black Mischief* and *Put Out More Flags*. At Balliol he was clever, handsome and good at languages. He was a fluent linguist as he had moved about a lot as a child due to his father's career. Self-assured and sophisticated compared with the other students, he was sent down from Oxford for entertaining women in his rooms after hours. His father sent him to Brazil to work in a bank, but he spent his spare time getting drunk and was given the sack. He was repatriated for being destitute. After that he tried banking in London, and journalism, and then went on an expedition to the Sahara for two years with his elder brother Francis. By 1933 he was working for an American bank in London.

Nancy respected Prod at first because he knew a lot of things and she was comparatively uneducated. He loved lecturing people and showing off his knowledge of facts on various obscure topics, regardless of whether or not his listeners were interested. He gave people lectures on topics such as lighthouses, the location of Atlantis, and lock keeping. When he went to ask Lord Redesdale for Nancy's hand in marriage he lectured him on the toll gates of England and Wales for two hours, which led to Nancy's younger sisters nickaming him 'The Old Toll-Gater'.

In December 1933 Nancy married Peter and they settled in London in a small house in Chiswick overlooking The Thames. While Peter was out at work during the day Nancy's friend Mark Ogilvie-Grant helped her with interior design, and they went round auction rooms together looking for bargains. Nancy liked the security of being married and having her own home. She bought two French bulldogs, whom she named Millie and Lottie, to keep her company, and enjoyed taking them out for long walks. Nancy and Peter enjoyed entertaining and gave a lot of bridge parties, but an early strain was put on their marriage when Peter left his job because he didn't like it. This left them short of money. They could have lived modestly on their allowances from both sets of parents and on Nancy's investments from the profits of her first two books, but Nancy liked good clothes and Peter liked expensive night clubs. So in the spring of 1934 Nancy started work on a new novel, *Wigs On The Green*. The plot revolves around the differences between a group of fascists and one of pacifists and features a girl called Eugenia who is based on Nancy's sister Unity. There is also a man called Captain Jack who is based on Diana Mitford's second husband Oswald Mosley. Nancy slipped a lot of private jokes into the novel, but Unity and Diana made her remove them before publication. They also forced her to cut out some scenes which they found offensive. The book was published virtually unnoticed by the reviewers in 1935.

In 1936 Nancy and Peter moved to a house in town in the area now known as Little Venice. Nancy enjoyed choosing new wallpaper and carpets, but Peter was drinking a lot and the Rodds weren't getting on. Peter went out drinking with male friends and started having affairs, but he did now have a job so at least they had some money. The following year saw Peter and Nancy intervening in a Mitford family crisis, though they failed to prevent the marriage of Nancy's younger sister, Jessica. In 1937 Jessica and her second cousin Esmond Romilly, a committed anti-fascist, had gone to to Spain where Esmond had managed to get a job reporting on the Spanish Civil War for the *News Chronicle*. Esmond, who was known by the media as 'Winston Churchill's Red Nephew' had earlier run away from Wellington College with his brother Giles and found work in a communist bookshop in London. Not long afterwards he joined the International Brigade to fight in Spain, but developed dysentery and was invalided out. While he was recuperating he met and fell in love with Jessica, who was also very ant-fascist, and persuaded her to go to Spain with him. Jessica pretended to her parents that she was going to Austria with some English friends. She and Esmond planned to marry in France on their way to Spain, but discovered initially that because they were both under age they needed parental permission. They moved on to Bilbao, where Esmond began his work as a correspondent and Jessica wrote to her mother to tell her that she was safe and would not be coming home.

Back in London the Mitford family met to discuss what to do, and it was decided that Peter and Nancy should go out to Spain to bring Jessica home. No doubt Peter had visions of himself being fêted as a hero, though it was through Winston Churchill, a relative of the Mitfords, that the Rodds' passage to St Juan de Luz in France (they had no visas to enter Spain) on a naval destroyer was organised. Jessica and Esmond were persuaded to meet Peter and Nancy in France. The story of the elopement of a peer's daughter was widely covered in the British press. The Rodds tried to persuade Jessica and Esmond to return to England and marry there, but they were unsuccessful and left France the next morning. Esmond managed to get a job with *Reuters* in Bayonne, where Lady Redesdale visited the pair but couldn't get them to go back to London. Letters from various relatives were also unsuccessful. Esmond eventually made an honest woman of Jessica on 18 May. Both mothers attended the civil wedding.

* * * * *

During the winter of 1937-8 Nancy was occupied in editing for publication two volumes of letters written by some of her Stanley ancestors. She enjoyed doing the research and reading the depictions of upper class English life written by cousins and other members of the family during the 19th century. In the preface, which was not printed when the books were re-issued after the war, Nancy has a conviction of the divine right of the English upper class to live in large houses and be waited on by servants. In the summer of 1938 Nancy became pregnant and wrote in great excitement to her old friend Robert Byron. Shortly afterwards, however, she suffered a miscarriage. By then Prod was out of work again and hoping to get a job at the BBC, but his elder brother Francis told them not to employ Prod because he was irresponsible. Nancy was furious (they desperately needed the money) and told Robert that she'd put Francis's name in a drawer (it was an old tradition in the Mitford family to put the names of people or animals one didn't like in a drawer, in the belief that that would make something bad happen to them).

In May 1939 Nancy joined Prod in Perpignan, where he was working for an international charity looking after refugees from the Spanish Civil War. There were so many refugees that the French authorities could not cope, and herded them into camps to be looked after by organisations such as the Red Cross. Nancy threw herself into voluntary work, which included arranging food, clothes, accommodation, and transport on refugee ships to Mexico, Morocco, and several places in France. Later she would write about her experiences in *The Pursuit of Love*, where Christian Talbot is a version of Prod. In the novel Christian is depicted as someone who is only interested in misery in the abstract, not in the plight of individual people. He is in his element with all those refugees to organise, and has no time for the petty concerns of the well-fed volunteers – he always assumes that everyone is happy and well unless they state otherwise. As Nancy could not speak Spanish and knew nothing about looking after children she was employed as a driver and odd job person. In *The Pursuit of Love* she portrays herself as Linda, Christian's wife, and describes delightfully the occasion when she assigns all the people with the word 'labrador' by their names to the best cabins on board the ship because she loves dogs. Christian is delighted at her egalitarianism, not realising that Nancy doesn't know that 'labrador' is Spanish for 'labourer'.

As soon as World War Two broke out Peter signed up and was given a commission in the Welsh Guards. In London Nancy worked on her next novel, *Pigeon Pie*. Her description of parliament makes it sound like an extension of Eton, except that the headmaster now delivers his lectures on the floor of the house instead of in chapel. The novel is set in the phoney war and likens the situation to that of children picking sides for a game which can't begin until the sides have been picked. England picks France and Germany picks Italy, then England chooses Poland and Germany retaliates by choosing Russia. England then picks Turkey and Germany chooses Spain. But Spain's nanny says that she can't play because she isn't well, Belgium has played the game before and hates it, and America thinks that she is too grown up to play such a babyish game.

The characters in the novel are based loosely on people that Nancy knew, with Sophia being Nancy herself, Luke representing Francis Rodd, the unreliable Rudolph playing Peter Rodd, and Sir Ivor King having all the attributes of Mark Ogilvie-Grant. Sir Ivor loves music hall songs, botany, and Greece. When Sophia asks him how the plants which he brought back from Lesbos are doing he complains about them being mere pansies.

After Peter had left for the Welsh Guards Nancy was desperately short of money and started taking in paying guests. They included her brother Tom, and Robert Byron. She began keeping hens and growing her own vegetables. She worked as a volunteer at a First Aid Post, but as it was the period of the Phoney War before the air raids began she had very little to do there. During 1940-41 Nancy found herself lonely and depressed. Most of her male friends were serving overseas, and in February 1941 Robert Byron was killed when the ship he was travelling on was torpedoed in the Atlantic. That same spring Nancy discovered that she was pregnant, but she again miscarried. After her recovery she took a job as a canteen assistant working with French soldiers, and began giving them English lessons. Teaching them English songs such as 'Come into the garden, Maud' revived her spirits. When the blitz began in September Nancy reckoned that her little house must be a favourite target of the Luftwaffe, and when she could no longer stand the nightly air raids she moved into the mews flat at the back of her parents' house in Rutland Gate. The main part of the house was being used to house families of Polish Jews evacuated from the East End, and Nancy flung herself wholeheartedly into helping to look after them.

But Nancy was again hard up, and needed to look for paid employment. Peter occasionally sent her a small cheque, but his father had died and his mother had stopped Nancy's allowance (Nancy reckoned she was using the money to build a ballroom in memory of her husband, and wished that her mother-in-law was religious because a mere marble bust would have cost far less). Peter visited London several times when he was on leave, but he stayed at his club and asked his friends not to tell Nancy that they had seen him. Their marriage was in effect over.

Nancy's private life then took a turn for the better. As she spoke French, she was asked by a friend at the War Office to infiltrate the Free French Officers' Club in London and find out what was going on there. She soon enjoyed dining with the officers at Emerald Cunard's suite in The Dorchester and at the Allies' Club in Park Lane, and as she was pretty and jolly she became very popular with the officers. She had a brief affair with one of them which resulted in an ectopic pregnancy, and while recovering was invited to stay with her friend Helen Dashwood at West Wycombe. Nancy's old friend James Lees-Milne was also staying there, and at weekends the house would be filled with other friends including such people as Cecil Beaton and Sibyl Colefax. When Nancy had recovered, James Lees-Milne suggested that she take a job at Heywood Hill's bookshop in Mayfair, and she started work there in March 1942. She was short of money and was grateful to be earning £3 10s a week. She left the shop at the end of the war but continued to correspond with Heywood Hill until her death in 1973. After Nancy moved to Paris she relied on Heywood Hill to provide her with interesting reading matter. In London she often walked home from the book shop to save the bus fare. One evening she forgot to lock up, and when she arrived the next morning the shop was full of people trying to buy books from each other. Wartime customers included such people as Cyril Connolly, Osbert Sitwell and James Lees-Milne. Harold Acton reckoned that many people went to the shop pretending to want a book but really wanting the pleasure of a chat with Nancy. Evelyn Waugh said that the shop was where the fashionable and intellectual met, at any rate, those who were still left in London.

Anyway, Nancy thoroughly enjoyed working there and her presence seems to have made the shop a success. She was also having more success in her private life, having met the Frenchman who would become the love of her life. Gaston Palewski (whom Nancy always referred to as The Colonel) was a member of the Free French and acting as de Gaulle's directeur de cabinet. He was an elegant Frenchman who was sophisticated, amusing, and a lover of the arts, and Nancy fell for him in a big way. She met him for the first time in September 1942, at the Allies' Club, when he had been asked to give her news of Peter and his brother Francis whom he had met while serving in Ethiopia. Nancy and Gaston discovered that they shared a love of France, French literature and French history, and a few days later Nancy invited Gaston to dine with her at home. The routine of dining together several evenings a week was soon established, the pair eating sometimes at The Connaught, sometimes at Nancy's home, and sometimes at the house in Eaton Terrace that The Colonel was renting from Anne Rosse. The Colonel, who spoke excellent English, loved to hear stories about Nancy's eccentric family, and he and Nancy were inseparable until he went to Algeria with de Gaulle in May 1943. Those nine months that Nancy and The Colonel spent together were quite possibly the happiest of Nancy's life. Nancy wrote to The Colonel frequently while he was in Algiers, and he occasionally wrote back, but although she continued her work in the bookshop her heart was not really in it. She went to parties with friends such as James Lees-Milne, Gerald Berners and Cecil Beaton, but life without The Colonel just wasn't the same. Then at last, in June 1944, The Colonel re-appeared in London for a week. His visit is poignantly described in *The Pursuit of Love*, where Linda revels in his presence and enjoys the small things such as the way he ties his tie and the sound of his voice. After the liberation of Paris in August 1944 The Colonel returned to his beloved city, and Nancy was left bereft.

Nancy's old friend Evelyn Waugh did his best to distract her at this time. He had just finished writing *Brideshead Revisited* and sent her the proofs to read. Nancy took a keen interest in the book, and when it was published she was gratified at the reception it received. She fed back to Evelyn the comments of various friends and critics, which included the fact that Raymond Mortimer thought it was a great English classic and Osbert Sitwell was jealous of the book's reception. Nancy longed to discuss the book with Evelyn in person, wanting to know all about his views on God and religion. Evelyn suggested that Nancy should take up writing again, and she began work on a semi-autobiographical novel, *The Pursuit of Love*.

* * * * *

By the time the Second World War ended in the summer of 1945 Nancy had had enough of working in a bookshop. Her father gave her £3,000 with which to buy a share in the shop and stock up on French literature, and in Autumn 1945 she went to Paris for two months, ostensibly to buy books for Heywood Hill but really to be near The Colonel. Accommodation in Paris was scarce, but The Colonel managed to find Nancy a room in a small hotel. The weather was good (there was an Indian Summer that year) and her beloved Colonel lived close by, and Nancy was determined that she would move to Paris for good. She was worried about running out of money, but Evelyn Waugh managed to arrange for her to write a weekly column on Paris for an American newspaper. In November she was obliged to return to London, where *The Pursuit of Love* was published on 10 December. The book sold 200,000 copies in twelve months, which enabled Nancy to leave the bookshop and return to Paris in April 1946.

At first Nancy stayed in cheap hotels or in friends' apartments while looking for somewhere to live and writing her next novel, *Love in a Cold Climate.* The book covers the same time frame as *The Pursuit of Love* but concentrates on a different set of characters (one *Guardian* critic described it as like a Greek tragedy rewritten by Noel Coward). The characters are again based on the lives of real people, though Cedric seems to be a composite of several of Nancy's gay friends. He is portrayed in a positive light and gains acceptance and success, becoming the heir to the Montdore house and name. Some of the episodes in Lady Montdore's life are based on things which happened to Violet Trefusis, but she also has elements of Lady Rennell, Nancy's mother-in-law. The Duc de Sauveterre, of course, is Gaston Palewski himself. The book sold well and was translated into several languages, though Nancy maintained that in Cairo the title had been translated as 'How to Make Love in the Cold' and that the book was included on lists of pornographic literature.

At the end of 1947 Nancy finally found a suitable apartment with a garden, which was on the ground floor of a house in Rue Monsieur. Thereafter she always referred to the apartment as 'Mr Street'. Here she was at last able to live the life for which she had yearned. Thanks to her writing she now had money to make the apartment comfortable and to buy antiques for it. Some of her antique furniture was sent out from London and restored lovingly by the French. Nancy was also able to buy nice clothes for herself, indulging in Dior's New Look which made her English clothes seem unutterably dowdy. She had an elderly maid to look after her and do the cooking, which was just as well as she was completely clueless – on one occasion in London when it was the servants' evening off they had left her some macaroni cheese with instructions to put it in the oven for 30 minutes, but when she took it out it was stone cold because they hadn't told her to turn the oven on. In Paris she enjoyed entertaining and being entertained. During her early years there she went to a lot of balls including several fancy dress ones given by Marie-Laure de Noailles which she loved dressing up for, but in later life she just enjoyed hearing about the balls.

Harold Acton likened Nancy's flat to a cultural annexe of the British Embassy, where the Duff Coopers had arrived in September 1944 and Diana had created a warm, welcoming atmosphere. Diana introduced Nancy to leading French artists, writers and musicians such as Cocteau and Poulenc. Nancy, perhaps unintentionally, set up a salon which rivalled that already established by Violet Trefusis, with the French considering Nancy a typical English aristocrat and her English friends thinking she was rather Frenchified. Violet, of course, had lived in Paris before the war and had written novels in both French and English. She knew many of the modernist painters, poets and musicians, as well as some leading politicians. She was not pleased to find that she suddenly had a rival hostess. Violet's mother was Alice Keppel and Violet always maintained that she herself was the illegitimate daughter of Edward VII. She was a terrific snob – the BBC's *Gloomsbury*, where she talks about the 'Sinjun Ambulance Brigade' captures her attitude in her younger years nicely. She spoke perfect French and derided Nancy's accent (Nancy's French later improved a lot when she learnt French clichés and idioms from listening to the radio). Violet had a total disregard for the niceties of English society and took the opportunity to call on Nancy one lunchtime. Nancy was just about to sit down to her lunch, a small portion of fish for one person, and felt obliged to ask Violet to join her. Violet scooped up the whole of the fish off the serving dish and put it on her own plate leaving Nancy with only vegetables to eat, an incident faithfully retold in *Love in a Cold Climate* when Fanny is entertaining.

Harold Acton recalled an occasion when Nancy got her own back on Violet. Derek Hill had done a portrait of Nancy's friend Princess Dolly Radziwill which was exhibited at the Leicester Galleries in London. Violet turned up at the private viewing and insisted on buying the original sketch for the painting, even though Dolly had never seen it. Derek had not wanted to sell it, and told Violet that if she gave it to Dolly for Christmas he would let her choose another of his paintings to keep instead. Dolly opened her Christmas present from Violet in front of a group of her friends, where Nancy told her that it was so unflattering that she would have to burn it. On another occasion when Violet was writing her memoirs she asked Nancy what she thought she ought to call them and Nancy said 'Here lies Mrs Trefusis'. Violet was not amused.

Once Nancy was established in Paris friends and relatives, including Hamish and Prod when they were passing through, came to visit between March and September each year. Nancy eventually divorced Prod in 1958 when he wanted to marry someone else. He died in 1968. Hamish sometimes stayed in hotels in Paris and called on Nancy, but she no longer found him attractive and disapproved of his extravagance. The Colonel came to dine from time to time. Nancy made occasional visits to friends such as L P Hartley, Anthony Powell and Evelyn Waugh in England, but found the houses of the gentry extremely cold and their food rather unpalatable compared with the French fare to which she became accustomed. She preferred to keep in touch with them by letter. She visited her parents on an annual basis and also stayed from time to time with other relatives. She enjoyed staying with her sister Debo both at Chatsworth and at Lismore Castle in Ireland. In the village shop at Lismore she once found a postcard of an old peasant in the style of Whistler and immediately sent off two dozen copies to various friends, saying that he looked just like Whistler's father.

Nancy also went to stay with friends who were living abroad. Every June she visited Mark Ogilvie-Grant in Greece, then in July she moved on to Venice where she stayed with her friend the Contessa Anna Maria Cicogna. Nancy's social circle in Venice included Victor Cunard, Somerset Maugham, the Chavchavadzes, the Graham Sutherlands and Cecil Beaton. On at least two occasions she also went to stay with Harold Acton in Florence. In France she made some new friends who included Madame Costa, the half sister of her mother's friend Mrs Hammersley. Madame Costa lived in an old manor house in the country at Fontaines les Nonnes not far from Paris, and Nancy used to stay with her for a few weeks every September. Sometimes she would retreat there to write in peace and escape from the constant visitors and 'phone calls at Rue Monsieur.

* * * * *

After the publication of *Love in a Cold Climate* in 1949 Nancy was much in demand, and *The Sunday Times* asked her to write a weekly column on life in Paris. She was also commissioned to do some translations, including *La Princesse de Cleves* by Madame de la Fayette and a play by Roussin translated as *The Little Hut.* The play had been running in Paris for three years, and Binkie Beaumont wanted to put it on in London. Described by Harold Acton as a bedroom farce transferred to the tropics, the play, with sets by

Nancy's old friend Oliver Messel, was performed in Edinburgh and Glasgow in the summer of 1950. Nancy attended some of the performances, and also went to the first night at the Lyric Theatre in London in August. She stayed with Mark Ogilvie-Grant in Kew, and the play was so successful that he gave a triumphant party in his home afterwards. Altogether there were 1,261 performances of *The Little Hut* at the Lyric. Nancy wondered what sort of people were going to see it, and when her cousin Bertrand Russell told her that he had been to watch it several times she decided that it must be old philosophers.

Nancy continued to write in order to fund her lifestyle, and her next novel, *The Blessing,* was published in 1951. The heroine, an English girl named Grace, moves to France and marries a French aristocrat who is a womaniser. The plot centres round the antics of the couple's son Sigismond, who plays each parent off against the other. Nancy could not resist a dig against America, which she detested, in the form of an American, Hector Dexter, who comes to Paris in connection with the Marshall Plan. The book sold well and the critics generally found it enjoyable, though they did not like the inference that everything French was more civilised than everything English. Nancy, by now a famous novelist, was asked to write regularly for *The Sunday Times,* but she had run out of ideas for plots for novels so her faithful correspondent Evelyn Waugh suggested that her next work should be a biography of a historical figure instead. Nancy, who loved history and enjoyed doing research, plumped for Madame de Pompadour, the mistress of Louis XV who influenced French politics for 20 years until she died at the age of 42. She was unsure whether to aim the book at historians or at the general reader, and Evelyn advised her to write for the sort of person who likes Louis XV furniture but thinks that Louis XV was the son of Louis XIV and had his head cut off.

Nancy recounts the tale as if it was a fairy story set in the wonderful palace of Versailles with good King Louis in charge and Madame de Pompadour bestowing favours on the poor and commissioning works of art. She chooses not to write about the more unsavoury aspects of the king's rule such as his ruthlessness, his oppression of his subjects, and the religious persecution. The book may not have presented all the historical facts, but it was a good read and full of interesting anecdotes and jokes. The manuscript was sent to Nancy's friend the literary critic Raymond Mortimer for him to check the historical and literary references. He found the style of the book peculiarly informal, saying it sounded as if someone was telling the story over the 'phone. The book was published in March 1954 with an elegant dust jacket designed by Cecil Beaton. Most historians didn't take it seriously. A J P Taylor thought it was just the characters from one of Nancy's novels reappearing in fancy dress, but it is included in the bibliography of Alfred Cobban's *History of Modern France*. Despite the criticisms the book sold well.

Nancy then embarked on a second literary biography, this time about the love affair between Voltaire and the Marquise du Châtelet. She had to do a lot more research for this second work, including reading many volumes of letters and visiting the Voltaire museum in Geneva. In order to avoid the constant telephone calls from friends and relations and get some peace and quiet in which to write up the research she retired to the island of Torcello in the Venetian lagoon for six weeks. *Voltaire in Love* was published in 1957. Between the two biographies, in 1955, Nancy wrote a jokey article published by Stephen Spender, which many people took seriously, and included an essay on the use of language by upper class (U) and non-U people. She instanced, for example, the use of looking glass, writing paper and luncheon as U, and mirror, note paper and lunch as non-U. She liked tradition and believed that everyone should know their place, and once said that she wanted cottagers to be happy in their cottages while she was happy in the Big House. Autre temps, autre moeurs. The article was reprinted as a book entitled *Noblesse Oblige* in 1956.

In October 1957 The Colonel was appointed French ambassador to Italy, and he lived in Rome until 1962. Nancy was devastated. She visited him in Rome once a year and he made the odd visit to Paris. They wrote to each other occasionally. In Autumn 1962 The Colonel was recalled to Paris and made Minister of State for Atomic Energy. Nancy was thrilled to have him back in Paris, despite his womanising and the fact that he had a mistress and an illegitimate son, but in March 1969 he married a rich woman who owned a beautiful château outside Paris.

* * * * *

After finishing *Voltaire in Love* Nancy had a rest from writing for a couple of years and then embarked on her final novel, *Don't Tell Alfred,* in August 1959. The novel is set in the British Embassy in Paris, Fanny and Alfred having moved there when Alfred was appointed ambassador. Their two drop-out sons and some other relations from previous novels cause havoc on the social scene, and Diana Cooper, the former ambassadress, appears as Lady Leone who can't bear to leave the embassy. The book was not well received by the critics but sold 50,000 copies in two months. It wasn't until 1964 that Nancy began writing her next book, a biography of Louis XIV called *The Sun King,* which is about the king who left great works of art. In September of that year she went to Fontaines for six weeks to begin writing it in peace. The writing came quickly and easily and the book was finished by January 1965. It was published by Rainbird ('L'Oiseau de pluie' in Nancy speak) as a coffee-table book, with illustrations of the king's pictures and the magnificent state rooms at Versailles, as well as portraits of the main characters. Some critics thought that Nancy had made the king seem too nice and had glossed over his shortcomings, but on the whole the reviews were good and the book sold 250,000 copies in two years. The enormous sales made Nancy a rich woman.

In January 1967 Nancy moved to a small house in Versailles with a large walled garden. She hadn't been seeing much of The Colonel as he had a new woman, and as the rent on her flat in Rue Monsieur had gone up sharply it seemed like a good time to move. Nancy had fallen in love with Versailles while researching Madame de Pompadour, and her new house was conveniently situated just a few minutes' walk from both the St Lazare and Les Invalides railway stations in Versailles. It was easy for Nancy, who did not have a car, to get up to town by train from there. Her large garden gave her a new hobby, and she consulted her botanising friend Mark Ogilvie-Grant about which plants to grow, while Alvilde Lees-Milne gave advice on growing roses. Birds and hedgehogs also began to feature prominently on Nancy's list of interests. Violet Trefusis had heard flattering reports about Nancy's new house and wanted to inspect it for herself. She rang up to invite herself to tea, but Nancy said that she would be out. Later Nancy heard rumours that Violet was terminally ill and so when Violet rang a second time she relented. Violet was 90 minutes late and horrid, according to her hostess.

In August 1968 Nancy started work on what would be her last book, a biography of the Prussian king Frederick The Great. She had already come across Frederick when she was researching Voltaire. Frederick was a patron of Voltaire and Nancy, who was fascinated by his personality, thought that it would be interesting to do some work on him. He seems an odd choice at first as Nancy didn't speak German, but

Frederick wrote and spoke in French and considered that German was only fit for horses. Neither of Nancy's two earlier publishers, Hamish Hamilton or George Rainbird, was keen to publish the book, especially as there was no love life to write about. Frederick seems to have had a penchant for young officers, but an appeal by Nancy to Peter Quennell, who was by then editor of *History Today*, was not enlightening on this subject. Rainbird later relented and agreed to publish the book as there were plenty of illustrations of Frederick's paintings and palaces which could be used in a coffee-table volume. So in November 1968 Nancy went to Prague to do some research on battles, and the following October she and her sister Pam, who spoke German, went to East Germany to visit battlefields, palaces and museums. *Frederick The Great* was published in 1970.

It was while researching her book on Frederick in the Spring of 1969 that Nancy began to suffer pain from the Hodgkin's Disease that would eventually kill her four years later. The excruciating pain affected both her back and her leg, but she tried to avoid painkillers as they befuddled her brain and she wanted to be able to write. After finishing Frederick she planned to write her memoirs, but in the end she was too ill to do so. The debilitating pain was to continue on and off for the last four years of Nancy's life. Sometimes there were periods of remission when she felt better for a few weeks, but these became fewer as the disease progressed. Nancy read a lot of books to distract herself from the pain, and writing letters to friends also helped. Sometimes she comforted herself by watching the birds in her garden. She saw many different doctors in both Paris and London, but it was only at the end of her life that her illness was diagnosed correctly. When she became helpless and bedridden her sisters and some of her friends including Billa Harrod and Alvilde Lees-Milne came in turns to look after her. She died on 30 June 1973 and was buried in the churchyard at Swinbrook.

CHAPTER TWO – MARK OGILVIE-GRANT

Mark Ogilvie-Grant (1905-1969) was educated at Eton and Trinity College, Oxford. Before World War Two he was a diplomat in Cairo, and after the war he lived and worked in Athens. He was a talented caricaturist and a keen amateur botanist.

* * * * *

Charles Randolph Mark Ogilvie-Grant (known as Mark) was born on 15 March 1905. He was the son of William Robert Ogilvie-Grant and Maud Louisa Pechell. He had three older sisters, Eleanora born in 1892, Marjorie born in 1894, and Alison born in 1896. The Scottish Ogilvie family from Cullen and the Grant family from Strathspey had been joined by marriage. Mark's father William, born in 1863, studied zoology with a private tutor and then went to work at the Natural History Museum, starting in the fish section. He later moved on to the Bird Room, eventually becoming the head of it. He also wrote books about birds and went on expeditions to various places including Madeira, the Azores and Dutch New Guinea. In 1916 he became paralysed due to illness, and in 1918 he retired and the family went to live in Reading. He died in 1924 and seems to have left Mark comfortably off.

Mark's education began at Wixenford Preparatory School where he soon encountered a like-minded boy called Harold Acton. They planned to start a museum together. Mark would provide Scottish exhibits and Harold would provide Italian items. They made lists of the things which they would collect for the museum. Mark's list included capercaillie eggs, dirks, tartans, and recipes for haggis. The nucleus of the museum consisted of things they collected on country walks such as a sheep's skull, a four-leaved clover, and some beetles. Later they added crystals, corals, birds' eggs and sea shells. During World War One the collection gained bullets and fragments of shells, bringing the museum more up to date. Nature study was Mark's main interest during these years but he was also keen on music and drawing. He became a chorister when he went to Eton. He used to sing solos and had such a good voice that it reduced some of the master to tears. Mark also did a lot of drawing but didn't join the club known as the Eton Society of Arts.

When he went up to Trinity College, Oxford, Mark continued to pursue his three main interests of botany, singing and drawing. He was a keen amateur botanist, his interest in the subject having begun at an early age when his father took him on trips to the Highlands to look at birds and butterflies. At Oxford Mark's old friend from Eton days, Robert Byron, introduced him to an undergraduates' drinking establishment known as the Hypocrites Club where they both sang and played the piano. Mark would sing Scottish Border ballads while Robert preferred Victorian ditties. On occasions Mark dressed as a cockney charlady and performed in a cockney accent, and he was also to be heard impersonating the contralto Dame Clara Butt singing 'Land of Hope and Glory'. In November 1924 Mark and Robert went to hear Dame Clara at the Albert Hall. Mark wrote her a note asking her to sing their favourite ballad, Hatton's Enchantress, and sent a small bunch of chrysanthemums on stage. He and Robert were absolutely thrilled when she obliged, and they stood up waving and shouting so that she would know from whom the request came. Mark also continued to indulge his love of drawing and became a talented caricaturist, practising on friends such as Robert, Evelyn Waugh and Harold Acton.

* * * * *

Mark probably first encountered Nancy Mitford at a dance at Eynsham Park, the home of the Mason family near Witney. Nancy and Mark got on very well because they shared the same puerile sense of humour. Mark enjoyed playing the fool, and Nancy found him amusing and enjoyed his company. He was soon being invited to house parties at Asthall Manor, the Mitford home, along with Nancy's other friends from Oxford University. Lord Redesdale, Nancy's father, approved of Mark because he liked shooting and was willing to get up early in the morning in order to take part in it. Most of Nancy's other male friends stayed in bed all morning when they visited, then spent the rest of the day lounging about the house and chatting. Lord Redesdale pronounced Mark's name as 'Muck', and at breakfast on one memorable occasion he went over to the sideboard, lifted the lid on one of the dishes and announced in a very satisfied voice "Brains for breakfast, Muck! Pigs' thinkers!". Poor Mark suddenly felt very queasy, and thereafter Nancy's young sisters would tease him by shouting "Brains for breakfast" at every possible opportunity.

Mark was a cousin of the heiress Nina Seafield. Nina had been friendly with Nancy since they met while attending débutante dances in London, and sometimes Mark, Nancy, and Nancy's fiancé Hamish Erskine would go and stay with Nina at her home, Cullen Castle in Scotland, where they would spend hours gossiping, drinking cocktails, and making fancy dress outfits. During the 1920s Mark and Nancy were two of the 'Bright Young Things' of the London scene, and they regularly attended fancy dress balls and cocktail parties with other friends such as Oliver Messel, Robert Byron, John Sutro, Brian Howard and Cecil Beaton. In May 1928 they went to the pageant of *Hyde Park Through The Ages*. Mark wore a white wig and knee breeches and Nancy thought he looked very fetching. This outfit gave her an idea for some of her stories - she would later go on to portray a wig-wearing character based on Mark in her short story *Two Old Ladies of*

Eaton Square, and in her novels *Wigs On The Green* and *Pigeon Pie*. The ladies in *Two Old Ladies of Eaton Square* are based on Nancy and her sister Diana, who were living together in Eaton Square after Diana had divorced her first husband, Bryan Guinness. In the story the ladies have an old male friend who wears a butter-coloured wig. He lives at the other end of the square but at one stage takes up with a pretty young woman who lives nearby and is based on Anne Armstrong-Jones, the sister of Nancy's friend Oliver Messel. Eventually the old man returns to the old ladies. In *Wigs On The Green* there is also an old gentleman who wears a butter-coloured wig (Nancy would subsequently refer to Mark as 'The Old Gentleman' when talking about him, and in her letters to him she often addressed him as 'OG' or 'Old' or simply 'Gentle'). The novel is a light-hearted send-up of the followers of British fascism. At a costume pageant the upper class fascists meet the locals, and a brawl between fascists and pacifists ensues. The characters in the novel include Miss Jones and Miss Smith, who are trying to escape a fiancé and a husband respectively, and a bored, married woman who thinks her lover is East European royalty when in reality he is an office worker with a small legacy. In *Pigeon Pie* Mark features as Sir Ivor King, whose wigless head is found on The Green. Sir Ivor is presumed dead and there is a Catholic Memorial Service (Mark was a Catholic). Then Sir Ivor's voice is heard broadcasting propaganda from Germany (the novel is set during World War Two) and it turns out that he has been kidnapped by The Boston Brotherhood, a religious cult which has been infiltrated by German spies. In the end it is revealed that Sir Ivor was spying on the Germans, and he is hailed as a great hero. Some of Nancy's other acquaintances also feature in the novel, with Lady Beech being based on her mother's friend Violet Hammersley, and her husband Peter Rodd featuring as Rudolph Jocelyn.

But life for Mark during the 1920s did not consist solely of partying. In April 1929 he was asked by the fashion magazine *Vogue* to produce the illustrations for an article about a ball being held in Palermo in Sicily. Cecil Beaton, who was by then a recognised photographer, was asked to take the photographs. The ball was held by the flamboyant Duc Fulco di Verdura, who had invited three hundred prominent people from Paris, London and New York to his Palazzo Verdura for a 1799 costume ball to honour the famous lovers Lord Nelson and Lady Hamilton. Many of the guests had commissioned period costumes from the major Paris couturiers. Mark's sketches of the guests were deemed a great success by *Vogue*, and he also illustrated light articles by both Nancy Mitford and Robert Byron for the magazine.

Mark went on to illustrate Nancy's first two novels, *Highland Fling* and *Christmas Pudding*. *Highland Fling* is set in a country house in Scotland and juxtaposes the Bright Young Things and the Old Fogeys. The main characters are Jane Dacre (based on Nancy herself) and her friend Albert Memorial Gates (based mainly on Robert Byron) who is a surrealist painter and prankster. Mark's caricature illustrations for the book included a drawing of a gentleman in a kilt actually doing the fling. Sadly, the drawings are no longer printed in modern editions of the novel.

Christmas Pudding is about a Christmas house party in a country house in the Cotswolds. The daughter of the house, Philadelphia, can't decide between two suitors. She has a brother, Bobby. Paul Fotheringay (based on Robert Byron again) pretends to be Bobby's tutor and comes to the house to write a biography of a Victorian poetess (Philadelphia's grandmother). But Philadelphia falls in love with Paul. Paul has written a serious novel and is deeply offended that it has been hailed as the funniest book of the year, as it was meant to be a tragedy.

In 1927 Mark took a break from partying and visited Mount Athos with Robert Byron and Robert's friends David Talbot Rice and Gerald Reitlinger. The reason for their visit was to photograph the frescoes in the monasteries, though Mark took the opportunity to draw some caricatures of the monks. He also enjoyed going for long walks with Robert, on which he saw strange butterflies and unusual insects. David was the chief photographer of the party, and Mark and Robert would sometimes sneak off while he was busy with his camera. On one occasion, while David was photographing a church in the small town of Caryes, Robert and Mark went to the feast of the Exaltation of the Cross at the Xeropotamou monastery and enjoyed some excellent food and wine (the normal fare at the monasteries was pretty Spartan). On his last night on Mount Athos, fed up of being bitten by bedbugs, Mark threw his hay-filled mattress out of the window. The mattress was later eaten by a donkey. After they had finished on Athos, David, Robert and Mark visited Mystra on the Greek mainland to photograph the frescoes in the many churches, then Robert and Mark went on to Crete and walked the famous Samaria gorge.

* * * * *

Life was not easy for a gay man in 1920s London, and by late 1929 Mark was living in Athens with his lover and companion Alastair Graham. Alastair had a diplomatic post, and had been living in Athens for some time. He had been a close friend of Evelyn Waugh's at Oxford. Evelyn, meeting up with Mark and Alastair while on his honeymoon cruise, found them happy and relaxed at no longer having to keep up the pretence of being straight. Evelyn's wife had fallen ill on the cruise, and he had accrued significant medical expenses as a result of this. He had run out of money, and Alastair kindly gave him some to tide him over. There are several conflicting accounts of the meeting between Evelyn and Alastair, with it being located variously in Port Said, Cairo, Cyprus and Athens. It seems mostly likely that Alastair went to Port Said to hand over the money, then when Evelyn's wife was well the Waughs visited Athens.

In 1930 Mark and Alastair moved to Cairo and Mark became an honorary attaché. Robert Byron, visiting Cairo in 1932, discovered that the British High Commissioner, Sir Percy Loraine, considered the pair lazy and wanted to replace them. He reckoned that one lady secretary would get through four times as much work as the pair of them, but despite this Mark managed to continue working in Cairo until 1941. During the 1930s he kept up a regular correspondence with his old friend Nancy Mitford, becoming her closest confidant. She wrote him long letters about her problems with her fiancé Hamish Erskine and gave him all the gossip about their mutual friends, and in return he told her about life in Egypt. They also shared private jokes. In December of 1930 Nancy wrote saying that she'd had lunch with Mark's mother and absent-mindedly shown her a letter from him in which he described the lift boy as a 'Driberg's delight'. It was not without difficulty that she managed to avoid explaining what was meant by that expression.

* * * * *

By 1941 Mark was working as attaché to the High Commissioner for Egypt and the Sudan. In September of that year he was sent from Cairo to Greece with the Special Operations Executive, but was taken prisoner almost as soon as he arrived in the Mani. There are conflicting versions of exactly what happened. One account has him parachuting into the Peloponnese, while others say that he was taken there by submarine from the Egyptian port of Alexandria, together with Alfred Lawrence of the Royal Tank Regiment, and told to make contact with a Greek agent codenamed Prometheus II. Yet another source has him being recruited to help with the spreading of disinformation, the disinformation including the fact that there was a British parachute regiment active in southern Greece. At any rate, he was captured by the Germans and sent to Austria as a prisoner of war. He escaped, but was re-captured after three weeks and sent to a camp in Germany. By May 1943 he was in a POW camp in Italy, but in March 1944 he was back in Germany. Nancy wrote to him regularly while he was imprisoned, in order to cheer him up. She told him that she took his wigs out every Sunday and shook them, but that the moths had been terrible that year. When he returned to London in April 1945 Nancy found him extremely thin but very cheerful. He said that he had been in about a dozen different POW camps, and that dreaming about the layer-cake with jam that he used to be given when visiting the Mitfords was one of the things which had kept him going.

After the war Mark returned to his house in Kew, where he loved to entertain his friends. He was an excellent cook and gave many dinner parties. Nancy used to lodge with him when her house in Blomfield Road was let, and after her move to Paris she stayed with him while working on parts of the dialogue for *Kind Hearts & Coronets* (none of her contributions made it into the final version of the film). In August 1950 Mark hosted another visit from Nancy when the play which she had translated from the French, *The Little Hut*, was on in London (it had previously toured Glasgow, Edinburgh and the provinces).

By 1953 Mark had settled permanently in Athens, where he worked for a petroleum company. He became fluent in Greek and translated two books into English - *Mosaic: A Greek Notebook* (published in 1959) and *Byzantium in the Seventh Century* (published in 1968). Mark loved cooking and entertaining, and his house became a centre for the ex-patriot community in Athens. English friends such as Evelyn Waugh would often stay with him, while others including Cecil Beaton and Dorothy Lygon (known as Coote) stayed in hotels but were entertained by Mark.

Mark's interest in botany continued for the rest of his life, and he spent his leave travelling round mainland Greece and its islands looking for interesting plant specimens. His trips often involved an element of adventure due to his absent-mindedness. In July 1958 he set off to visit the island of Paros with his friend Patrick Leigh-Fermor, Patrick's wife Joan, Maurice Bowra from Oxford, and a friend of Bowra's, the German historian Ernst Kantorowicz. They set off by ferry and arrived en route to Paros at the island of Syra. Patrick and Mark went ashore and started drinking at a taverna. They had some kebabs, then some more kebabs, and while they were still in the taverna the ferry left without them. On finding that there would not be another boat to Paros for two days they were wandering unhappily along the quayside when they stopped to admire a yacht. By an amazing co-incidence it turned out to belong to their friend Lord Antrim, who was also visiting Syra, and they arrived on Paros in style the next morning.

Nancy Mitford visited some of the islands with Mark on his botanical expeditions. Sometimes they stayed with the Leigh-Fermors, at first on the island of Hydra and later at their homes in Euboea and Kardamyli. On one occasion when Mark and Nancy were staying on Hydra the Leigh-Fermors were looking after a neighbour's dog called Spot. The dog would not stop barking when some friends called round. Nancy, whose wit was as sharp as ever, could not resist exclaiming "Out, damned Spot!".

Mark and Nancy wrote each other long letters from their respective homes in Athens and Paris, and after Nancy moved to a house with a garden at Versailles she asked for advice on how to propagate poppies and cornflowers, and on how to care for her tortoise. Mark often stayed with her in

Paris and Nancy was a regular visitor to Greece, usually spending a few weeks there in June each year before going on to Venice. Mark took her to the ancient sites of Olympia and Delphi, and in the Spring of 1960 he went to Delphi again with Nancy's sister Deborah and her husband Andrew and daughter Emma. The Devonshire family were on a Hellenic cruise and had arranged to meet up with Mark near Delphi. Mark took Andrew and Emma on a walk in the mountains, got lost in his typical absent-minded way, and the cruise ship left without them. For years afterwards passengers on the ship were warned not to stray like the Duke of Devonshire. The following October Mark again visited the Delphi area, this time with Patrick Leigh-Fermor. Mark was on one of his botany expeditions, looking for unusual plant species, and he had a trowel and polythene bag with him. Again he lost his bearings. The pair became thirsty, and when Mark bent over a well in order to see whether the bucket was coming up, the pair of spectacles which he kept in his breast pocket fell straight down the well.

Mark's life was a happy and fulfilled one, but not a long one. Nancy's last letter to him was written in November 1968. Shortly after that he was diagnosed with cancer and returned to London for treatment. He died in January 1969.

CHAPTER THREE – JAMES LEES-MILNE

James Lees-Milne (1908-1997) has been described as 'the man who saved England'. He was an expert on country houses who worked for the National Trust from 1936-73, and was more or less single-handedly responsible for persuading many owners to give their properties to the National Trust. He was also an architectural historian and biographer, and his twelve volumes of published diaries provide a fascinating insight into his life and work.

* * * * *

George James Henry Lees-Milne (who was known as Jim) was born on 6th August 1908. Both his parents came from families which had made their fortunes in industry during the 19th century and then become minor landed gentry. Two years before his birth his parents purchased Wickhamford Manor, a mediaeval manor house near Evesham in Worcestershire. Jim was the middle one of three children. His sister Audrey was three years older than he was, and his brother Richard, known as Dick, was two years younger. His parents led separate lives from each other and didn't have much to do with their children. Jim had a lonely childhood and spent much of the school holidays sitting in the garden reading books. He didn't have much in common with his siblings (in adult life his brother Dick, although younger than Jim, was chosen to run the family cotton mill in Lancashire). Jim hated his philistine father and didn't see much of his mother. His parents liked field sports and were not interested in the arts - his father thought that if someone was referred to as 'artistic' it meant that they had unnatural vices. The children's friends were the children of their parents' sporting friends, with whom they would go riding and play tennis. They enjoyed visiting their neighbours at Bretforton Manor, and also the Eyres-Monsell family at Dumbleton Hall. Graham Monsell would go to Eton with Jim, and his sister Joan would later marry the writer Patrick Leigh-Fermor. The Eyres-Monsell parents were hunting friends of the Lees-Milnes. The family also spent holidays with various relatives in Scotland and Wales.

Jim's mother was often away on vacation with one or other of her various lovers when he was at home during the school holidays. In his hilarious autobiography, *Another Self*, he recalls an incident when his mother took him to meet one of them, a balloonist, at Broadway Hill. According to Jim the lovers sailed away in a balloon, benevolently scattering one-pound notes and leaving him to explain to his father why there would be one fewer for lunch that day, but in real life the lover appears to have been an aviator. As with other incidents recorded in *Another Self*, the details seem to have been exaggerated for comic effect.

From January 1919 - July 1921 Jim attended Lockers Park Preparatory School. Edward James, Peter Watson and Guy Burgess were contemporaries. The emphasis was on games and classics, as in most similar establishments. Jim shared a dormitory with four other boys, one of whom, Tom Mitford, would become a lifelong friend.

* * * * *

In September 1921 Jim and Tom Mitford both started at Eton. Jim joined McNeile's house, the connection being that his mother had been at finishing school with McNeile's wife. McNeile was an austere character who was very strict. Michael Rosse and his younger brother Desmond Parsons were also in McNeile's, though Desmond was two years younger than Jim and Michael was three years older. Both of them would later become friends of Jim. Desmond was considered one of the most beautiful boys in the school and several of the other boys had crushes on him. A sketch of him by fellow Etonian William Acton does indeed portray him as very handsome and looking like a girl. Jim's brother Dick later also joined McNeile's.

When Jim was fifteen he was seduced by one of the older boys in the house, and he went on to have affairs with both Tom Mitford and Desmond Parsons. Affairs had to be carried out discreetly, as they would result in expulsion if uncovered. In *Another Self* Jim talks about lying in the long grass with Desmond Parsons, and in his diaries he remembers passionately embracing Tom Mitford at the entrance to Eton chapel when no-one could see them. From the age of 10 or 11 Jim would spend part of his holidays at Asthall Manor with the Mitford family, and he got to know all of Tom's sisters. The Mitfords shared his love of books and music, and he read a lot of poetry with the sisters. It was very different from his own home life, where his father was not interested in the arts and there were no books. He became very fond of Diana, who was two years his junior, and later likened her to a Botticelli Venus.

At Eton Jim was only of average academic ability. He hated games and was allowed to take rowing instead of cricket. He didn't distinguish himself in any way and had no wish to do so. Most of his spare time was spent reading in the school library. He read a lot of Victorian novels and poetry, devouring Thackeray, Shelley and Swinburne. Two boys who shared his love of literature and became his friends were Alan Pryce-Jones and Rupert Hart-Davies. Pryce-Jones would go on to become editor of the *Times Literary Supplement*, and Hart-Davies became a publisher, editor, and prolific letter writer. Pryce-Jones introduced Jim to a secret club which met at the back of a teashop in Eton High Street. The members read forbidden books, listened to gramophone records and drank cocktails.

In December 1925 Jim passed the School Certificate examination and in July 1926 he left Eton. His father didn't want him to go to university and thought that Jim ought to earn his living, though he did give him a year or so to think about what he wanted to do. Jim visited Italy, France and North Africa with his mother, then for the first half of 1927 he studied at the University of Grenoble, which specialised in French courses for foreigners. In October 1927, at the instigation of his father, Jim started a six-month secretarial course in London. He was the only male on the course, and was taking it because his father thought the course would be useful preparation for a business career. He learnt shorthand and typing, but wasn't cut out to go into business. His father gave him an allowance of ten shillings a week, out of which he had to buy his lunches. He couldn't afford bus or tube fares so walked everywhere, which gave him ample opportunity to study the architecture of the buildings he passed.

By the time Jim was 20 his father had realised that he would never make a successful businessman, and he allowed Jim to go to Magdalen College, Oxford, to read History. At Oxford Jim met and became friends with Randolph Churchill, John Betjeman and Osbert Lancaster, and developed a love of poetry and architecture. Alan Pryce-Jones was a fellow student at Magdalen. At some weekends and during some university vacations Jim and a selection of fellow students would descend on the Mitford family, who by then were living in Swinbrook near Burford. Lord Redesdale, the father of the Mitford children, was shocked by the behaviour of the friends, whom he considered ridiculously effeminate. His opinion of them was not improved when on one occasion a comb fell out of Jim's pocket. Another time when Jim was staying at Swinbrook he expounded his pro-German views at the dinner table and Lord Redesdale stormed out of the room. Nancy and her sisters told Jim that he ought to leave. According to Nancy's account of the incident it was raining heavily that evening and Jim's motorbike refused to start, so he sneaked back into the house via the servants' entrance and left the next morning. According to *Another Self*, when Jim went back into the house he was welcomed by Lord Redesdale, forgiven, plied with drink, and allowed to stay on for another week. Lord Redesdale was at heart a kind and forgiving man, though Jim's version of the incident should probably be taken with a large pinch of salt.

In *Another Self* Jim goes on to describe a drunken party he attended with fellow undergraduates at Rousham, a Jacobean house near Oxford. The house had Rococo rooms with delicate furniture, and was let to a rich alcoholic called Maurice Hastings. Maurice's family owned *The Architectural Review*, and it was through him that John Betjeman would later get a job on that journal. Maurice, who was drunk, fired a rifle at the statues and cracked a hunting whip at some of the pictures, damaging Reynoldses and Knellers. Jim, who loved art and architecture, maintained that it was this incident which made him want to dedicate himself to preserving country houses. There is some doubt as to whether Jim himself was actually present (Roy Harrod, who was, had no recollection of Jim being there) but the incident was widely discussed in Oxford so he would undoubtedly have heard about it. At any rate, it seems to have sparked his desire to look after country houses and their contents.

* * * * *

In 1931 Jim, like many of his contemporaries, came down from Oxford with no money and a third class degree. Unlike most of his fellow graduates, however, he needed to earn a living, so he took the entrance examinations for both the diplomatic service and the home civil service. Having failed both of those he enrolled with a London secretarial agency and in January 1932 secured a job as secretary to Lord Lloyd.

His employer had been Governor of Bombay from December 1918 - December 1923 and then High Commissioner in Egypt from 1925-29. Lloyd was active in Conservative politics and was an opponent of the National Government. He was busy opposing home rule for India, and he was also writing a book about Egypt. As well as this he had several business interests. Jim's duties included keeping Lord Lloyd's diary, taking dictation for his daily letters, typing up drafts of his speeches and newspaper articles, acting as secretary for the Egyptian book, and doing the filing. When Lord Lloyd was away on business Jim had to deal with his correspondence. Lord Lloyd paid for Jim to have a summer holiday each year, which enabled him to visit Portugal, Majorca and Corsica.

During the 1930s Jim kept up with his old friends from Eton and Oxford, many of whom were now living and working in London. He also became better acquainted with a group of slightly older men who used to return to Oxford to visit friends while he was an undergraduate. The group included Harold Acton, Robert Byron, Brian Howard, Patrick Balfour, Cyril Connolly, John Sutro, and Peter Quennell. Jim often used to meet up with them at the Café Royal, which was a useful venue for relatively impoverished people to meet those from the literary and art world. Some of his acquaintances also invited him to weekend country house parties. Several times he stayed with the Bryan Guinnesses (Bryan had married Diana Mitford in 1929) at Biddesden, and he also visited Johnnie Churchill at his home near Marlborough. From both locations parties would visit Robert Byron and his family at nearby Savernake Lodge where Robert's mother, who was very sociable, loved to entertain his friends. Jim also met people at débutante dances during The Season, and made some new friends such as George Chavchavadze (the pianist who was descended from the kings of Georgia), Paul Latham (an MP who had inherited Herstmonceux Castle from his industrialist father), and Midi O'Neill who was a friend of

Nancy Mitford. In 1934 Midi married Derick Gascoigne. The Gascoignes would become the parents of the Bamber Gascoigne of *University Challenge* fame.

It was also during the 1930s that Jim became the lover of Harold Nicolson. Jim first met Harold when they were both campaigning for Oswald Mosley in Stoke at the General Election of October 1931. Mosley was standing as a candidate for the New Party. Jim's Aunt Dorothy's sister Maud was the mother of Oswald Mosley, and she persuaded Jim to help with the electoral campaign. Harold Nicolson was a member of the New Party and the editor of the New Party's newspaper and was helping with the campaign. By that time the Nicolsons were living mainly separate lives, with Harold's wife Vita Sackville-West devoting herself to gardening at their home, Sissinghurst, and Harold living in London during the week and only visiting Sissinghurst at weekends. During the first half of the 1930s Harold was busy with his writing, which included books on the Paris Peace Conference and Lord Curzon. He had given up being a diplomat as Vita refused to accompany him on foreign postings. In February 1934 Jim accompanied Harold to Paris for a romantic weekend. Harold was on his way to stay with Vita in Italy (Vita was staying in Portofino with Harold's sister, with whom she was having an affair). Harold showed Jim round Paris and they visited The Hall of Mirrors at Versailles, where Harold had witnessed the signing of the 1919 peace treaty when he was a member of the British delegation at the Paris Peace Conference. Jim also met James Joyce, whom Harold knew, and was absolutely thrilled to make the acquaintance of such a famous writer.

Towards the end of 1934 Jim, who had previously lived in a succession of bedsits, became Harold's lodger and lover. Through Harold he met the literary set which included Raymond Mortimer, Eddy Sackville-West and James Pope-Hennessy. Jim's later desire to keep a diary seems to have been fuelled in part by him watching his mentor typing up his own diary every evening.

Almost without him realising what was happening, in April 1935 Jim became engaged to Anne Gathorne-Hardy, the sister of the rare book dealer Eddie Gathorne-Hardy. Jim had met Anne a few weeks earlier when they were both staying with the Johnnie Churchills in Oxfordshire. Anne was a cousin of Johnnie's wife Angela, and although she was not beautiful Jim was attracted to her because of her lively mind and good sense of humour. She came from an intellectual family and Jim seems to have fallen in love with her at first sight, though the attraction for her seems to have been the possibility of escaping from a narrow home life. She seems a rather odd choice for Jim, as she shared her mother's left-wing and atheist views (Jim was by this time a devout Catholic, having been received into the Catholic Church in March 1934. He had chosen Catholicism because he liked the Latin litany and the ceremony and incense that went with it, as well as the unbroken tradition. There were also other reasons for his choice of religion – he saw the Catholic Church as a bulwark against Communism, and he knew that his becoming a Catholic would annoy his father. A third reason seems to have been that the literary scene between the wars included many Catholics. His friends Alan Pryce-Jones, Hamish Erskine and Eddy Sackville-West also converted, although Jim disliked Graham Greene and Evelyn Waugh, whom he considered to be drunks. He did, however, admire the converts G K Chesterton and Ronald Knox).

After they were engaged Jim and Anne wrote to each other almost daily, but they did not meet very often. Anne was very shy, and when she accompanied Jim to parties given by his friends she was overawed by people like Nancy Mitford and her acquaintances and hardly spoke. Jim had made it clear to Anne from the outset that they would not be able to get married until he was earning enough money to support them both. In June 1935 he left Lord Lloyd and took a job as an assistant to the head of Reuters, Sir Roderick Jones, apparently because he wanted more money on which to marry. It was a lowly position in the news agency and Jim, who hated the job, had to do such things as shopping and arranging car insurance for Sir Roderick. Sir Roderick was a bully and often kept Jim late at the office taking down dictation or retyping his mistakes.

After six months Jim and Sir Roderick parted company. In *Another Self* Jim fantasises about handing in his notice and telling Sir Roderick what he thinks of him, but the reality seems to have been that Sir Roderick decided to dispense with Jim's services because he had decided that he didn't fit in at Reuters. Jim was still living with Harold and enjoying his bachelor lifestyle, while Anne was safe in the country with her mother. He had been having doubts about whether he ought to get married at all due to his innate homosexuality, and in January 1936 he used his lack of money as an excuse to break off the engagement. Anne would later go on to marry the bookseller Heywood Hill in 1938.

* * * * *

Jim was lucky in having connections, and in February 1936 Harold Nicolson got him a job interview at the National Trust. In Spring of that year Jim was appointed secretary to the Country Houses Committee of the Trust. The committee had just been created, the National Trust having been concerned mainly with land rather than buildings up to that point. Harold had been able to secure the post because a former lover of Vita's was the sister of Donald Matheson, the National Trust's secretary.

Jim's task was to compile a list of houses deemed worthy of preservation and persuade the owners to give them to the National Trust. Death duties had risen to fifty per cent and many houses were in danger of falling into disrepair because their owners could not afford to maintain them. The plan was for families who owned large houses to remain in situ after the houses were handed over to the Trust, but they were expected to provide large endowments and to open their houses to the public for at least thirty days each year. Smaller houses would open as museums and would not have anyone living in them.

Jim started work for the National Trust with a small salary, no car and no expenses allowance. His job therefore necessitated taking his bicycle on the train to the railway station nearest to the house he was visiting, and cycling the rest of the way. He was an amateur historian who learnt about architecture, furniture and pictures as he went along. There were hardly any reference books in those days, so he made his own notes for future use. Many of the houses he visited turned out to be of little architectural merit. Lots of them had extensions or additions which were not in keeping with the original house, and they often had badly restored façades or nasty Edwardian additions. Jim was always diplomatic, polite and tactful. He tried to find something nice to say to the owners about the houses he rejected, for example that they were charming but not quite what the Trust was looking for. He explained that the houses had to be considered by a committee and so he couldn't make a decision there and then about whether to accept them. The owners of the houses fell broadly into two categories - those who were pleasant and welcoming but whose houses were not suitable to become National Trust properties, and those whose houses were just the type the Trust was looking for but who were either unable or unwilling to provide sufficient endowment. Some of the owners were so grumpy and suspicious that they wouldn't even let Jim through the front door. The upshot of all this was that although Jim visited hundreds of houses, very few of them were accepted by the Trust between 1936 and the outbreak of the Second World War.

Between 1936 and 1939 Jim concentrated on domestic architecture and socialised almost exclusively with others who cared about it too such as John Betjeman and Robert Byron, both of whom he had known since his Oxford days. In the Spring of 1937 Robert was instrumental in founding the Georgian Group for the protection of Georgian architecture. The Group started as a sub-committee of the Society for the Protection of Ancient Buildings (SPAB) but in Autumn 1937 became independent from it. Jim was on the committee of the Georgian Group and spent much of his spare time working for it. Also on the committee were his old friends John Betjeman, Osbert Lancaster and Michael Rosse.

Although architecture was taking up most of his time by then, Jim's love life was not entirely in abeyance. On 1st March 1938 he fell in love with Rick Stewart-Jones who was working for SPAB, and the two of them went on to have a passionate affair. They first met when Jim was representing the National Trust and Rick was representing SPAB, at a house in Queen Anne's Gate which had been offered to the Trust. Rick, who was always late for everything, arrived after Jim had already let himself in with the key and locked the front door, so Rick shinned up a drainpipe and broke a window to get in. Jim, expecting a burglar, was confronted by a gorgeous young man. It was love at first sight. Rick had bought some houses in Cheyne Walk and was in the middle of a project to restore them. One of them was a house with a 1750s ballroom. The house had at one stage been the home of the artist Whistler and was sold to Rick by Bryan Guinness, who apparently let it go cheaply because he approved of Rick's project. Rick let rooms in part of the house to friends at a very reasonable rate, and he rented out the ballroom for parties. Some of his relatives also lived in the house. It was not a conventional household and there were a lot of lodgers including several couples who were living in sin. Jim moved in with Rick not long after he had met him, and they lived together until the outbreak of the war except for a period of a few weeks when Robert Byron persuaded Jim to leave 'that refined brothel' and move in with him. Robert, who had fancied Jim for some time, was renting an elegant Georgian house nearby, complete with a manservant. Jim found Robert too neurotic (a few years earlier Harold Acton had found the same thing when lodging with him) and he soon moved back to the chaos of Cheyne Walk. Life with Rick had its ups and downs, and Jim soon discovered that Rick was very unreliable and unpunctual. Rick was a local councillor who took his duties very seriously, and he often went off at the last moment to attend to the poor and needy even though he had prior engagements with Jim. Love seems to have triumphed despite this, however.

* * * * *

In September 1939 the work of the Country Houses Committee was suspended and Jim's job at the National Trust came to an abrupt end. A pacifist by nature, he trained as an ambulance driver, but early in 1940 Robert Byron persuaded him that it was his duty to enlist. 'What would happen if everyone in this country was a pacifist ?' he asked. In Spring 1940 Michael Rosse arranged a commission for Jim in the Irish Guards, and he spent six months training. In September he was posted to Dover, where he seems to have had great difficulty in mastering the commands needed to drill his men successfully. According to *Another Self* Jim didn't know the command for 'stop' and the men, trained to obey commands, carried on walking and marched over the edge of a cliff. One presumes it didn't happen quite like that in reality.

In October of that year Jim was caught in a bomb blast in London and he spent the next twelve months in and out of military hospitals. Eventually he was diagnosed with Jacksonian epilepsy and discharged from the military on medical grounds. Jim's diaries and letters give a good account of what daily life was like in London during the blitz. He led a frantic social life and kept up with friends such as the Rosses and Harold Nicolson. He also spoke regularly to a mystery lady on the 'phone, whom he first encountered due to a crossed line. They got on so well that he would often ring her late at night to discuss Balzac and other literary figures, but he never found out who she was. *Another Self* gives a no-doubt exaggerated account of these conversations.

The National Trust was revived in Autumn 1941 and its headquarters relocated to West Wycombe, a large Palladian house in Buckinghamshire which was the home of John and Helen Dashwood. Many country houses were requisitioned by the military, and their owners were wondering how to preserve them after the war. The Dashwoods, however, managed to avoid having their house requisitioned by saying that they were taking in refugees. The evacuees were mostly friends of Helen, and included an invalid Nancy Mitford, Eddy Sackville-West, and Clementine Beit. At weekends other friends such as Cecil Beaton and Sibyl Colefax would come and stay. Jim's job at the National Trust was revived, and he became one of the West Wycombe residents. The Wallace Collection had also been evacuated there. In the evenings Nancy, Jim and Eddy enjoyed sitting round the fire gossiping about their friends and knitting items for the war effort (Clementine reckoned that the sock Jim was knitting would unravel on St. Milne's day). Nancy developed an interest in Captain Scott and made all the others read about him too. She started referring to the lavatory at West Wycombe as the Beardmore after a glacier which Scott had encountered, because it was so cold in there that it reminded her of the Arctic. She would later base two of the characters in *Love in a Cold Climate* on people at West Wycombe - Helen became Lady Montdore and Eddy was immortalised as Davey the hypochondriac.

It was while he was living at West Wycombe that

Jim started writing the diary which he would maintain for the rest of his life. He thought that writing about one's day was the next best thing to having someone to share things with. Edited versions of his diaries were gradually published over the years, and they make fascinating reading because he met so many interesting people. For many years the National Trust refused to stock the diaries in their shops because of the things he said about some of the owners of the country houses he visited.

By the Spring of 1942 Nancy had recovered from her ectopic pregnancy. She returned to London and got a job at Heywood Hill's bookshop. Jim himself moved to London shortly afterwards when the National Trust returned to Buckingham Palace Gardens. Rick Stewart-Jones pointed out that the house next door to his in Cheyne Walk was for sale, and Jim managed to buy it very cheaply. From 1942-45 he travelled round Britain visiting many country houses and met lots of eccentric owners about whom he wrote in his diaries. They included Lord Berwick of Attingham who thought that ghosts were living in his vacuum cleaner, Lady Sibyl Grant who was living in a tree house because she thought that her home, Pitchford Hall, was haunted, and Lord Berners of Faringdon House who lived in a household consisting of himself, his boyfriend Robert Heber-Percy, and Robert's wife and daughter.

* * * * *

Important houses which Jim managed to secure for the National Trust during war time include :-

1942 **Cliveden** in Buckinghamshire. This house was given to the National Trust with the proviso that the Astor family could continue to live there as long as they wanted. It had an enormous endowment of £250,000 given by its owner Lord

Astor. The house had been designed by Sir Charles Barry in 1851 and replaced an older house on the site which had been destroyed by fire in 1849. Waldorf Astor inherited the house from his wealthy American father, the 1st Lord Astor, when he married Nancy Langhorne in 1906. After Waldorf entered the House of Lords Nancy stood for parliament in 1919 and was Conservative MP for Plymouth Sutton until 1945. She was the first female member of parliament. Waldorf and Nancy used the huge house and grounds for entertaining in the 1920s and 1930s and had enormous house parties staying. Famous world leaders, politicians and artists used to stay there including Churchill, Gandhi, George Bernard Shaw, Edith Wharton, Roosevelt, Asquith and Henry James. Harold Nicolson (who visited in the 1930s) thought that living at Cliveden would be like living on the stage at La Scala. The Astor family left Cliveden in 1968, shortly after the Profumo Affair. Since 1984 Cliveden has been run as a hotel. It has been restored and filled with Edwardian antiques so looks similar to the way it would have been when Nancy Astor lived there. The gardens and grounds are open to the public and it is also possible to have a guided tour of a small part of the house.

1942 **Polesden Lacey**, a Regency house and its contents and estate in Surrey. The house was extensively altered in 1906 by the society hostess Mrs Ronnie Greville. Her father had made his fortune in the brewing industry, and became a Liberal MP in 1886. Her husband was a friend of Winston Churchill. She gave lavish parties at which she entertained international royalty, politicians, and such people as the Rothschilds and the Sassoons. About her friend the deposed king of Greece she said "I love him even though he is an ex-king". She was a close friend of Queen Mary and left her jewellery to Queen Elizabeth The Queen Mother. Her husband died in 1908 but she continued to entertain on a large scale. The house had an extensive collection of furniture, porcelain, silver and art. Mrs

Greville had no children and left her estate to the National Trust on her death in 1942.

1943 **Knole** in Kent. This is one of the five largest houses in England and was the childhood home of Vita Sackville-West. On the death of her father it passed to his brother Charles, who was the father of Eddy Sackville-West. Vita wished she had been born a boy so she could inherit Knole, and Eddy wished he had been born a girl so he didn't have the responsibility of it. Most of the endowment came from the estate of Mrs Ronnie Greville.

1944 **Lindisfarne Castle** in Northumberland. The castle came with an enormous endowment. Jim was not keen on the 16th century building because it had been modernised, but accepted it because of the endowment. In 1901 it had been bought by Edward Hudson, the founder of *Country Life* magazine, who refurbished it in the Arts & Craft style at the instigation of the architect Sir Edwin Lutyens. The garden was designed by Gertrude Jekyll.

1945 **Charlecote Park** in Warwickshire. In 1936 the eccentric owner, Sir Henry Fairfax-Lucy, had refused to show Jim round the house. Over the next eight years Sir Henry enjoyed making various offers to the National Trust and then withdrawing them at the last moment. He died in 1944 and in 1945 his children gave the house to the Trust, though there was virtually no endowment. It is a 16th-century house with grounds which were landscaped by Capability Brown in about 1760. Queen Elizabeth I stayed there, and there is a contemporary painting of her in the Great Hall.

* * * * *

In 1945 Jim combined his work for the National Trust with visiting Adam houses for his first book, which was about the

Scottish architect Robert Adam. Very little had been written about Adam for the general reader. Jim visited houses such as Syon Park and also other buildings in London which had been designed by Adam. He didn't approve of what had happened to some of the London houses, flying into a rage, for example, about Lansdowne House whose drawing room was on display in the Philadelphia Museum of Art. *The Age of Adam* was published in 1947.

It was also during the war that Jim had an affair with the writer James Pope-Hennessy, whom he met through Harold Nicolson. Harold first met James, who was at Balliol College Oxford with his son Nigel, in August 1936. Nigel had been in love with James, but Harold found him gorgeous and quickly seduced him. Jim was introduced to James at this time and they had an on-off affair that lasted more than ten years. They shared a love of architecture, and in 1937 James's mother helped Jim to plan a country houses exhibition in aid of the National Trust. The Pope-Hennessys were devout Catholics, which was one of the reasons that Jim was attracted to them. James's elder brother, John, an art historian, would later become Director of the Victoria & Albert Museum (1967-73) and Director of the British Museum (1974-76). James himself wrote books on architecture, travel books, and biographies of people including Queen Mary and Anthony Trollope (the character of Phineas Finn was based on James's grandfather). James was always short of money, and in October 1949 he rang Jim to say that he'd sold the picture of an 18th-century house which he had been intending to leave Jim in his will. If Jim wanted to buy it he could go to Appleby's, where it was on display in the window. James, who drank heavily, went on to became an alcoholic, frequented seedy London bars, and was murdered in 1974 by 'rough trade'.

* * * * *

In 1945 Jim was appointed Secretary of the Historic Buildings Committee. At first he worked on his own, but in 1947 regional representatives were appointed to help him. Between 1945 and 1951 he acquired many important houses for the National Trust. He organised repairs, arranged the furniture, saw to the openings and wrote some of the guide books. Other guide books were written by the owners of the houses themselves. His diaries for this period provide a fascinating glimpse of how the houses were arranged ready for opening to the public. Houses with which Jim was involved include :-

1946 **Coughton Court**. A Tudor country house in Warwickshire. The Throckmorton family have a 300-year lease on the house. The estate has been owned by the Throckmorton family since 1409, and the house is famous for its connection with a plot to murder Queen Elizabeth I in 1583. The family were Catholics and sheltered some of the conspirators of the Gunpowder Plot in 1605. Jim befriended Sir Robert Throckmorton's mother, who persuaded her son to hand over the house to the Trust.

1946 **Montacute House.** An Elizabethan manor house in Sussex which was empty at the time. The house had been let to a succession of tenants, including Lord Curzon who lived there with his mistress. The descendants of Sir Edward Phelips, who built the house, lived there until the early 20th century. During World War Two American soldiers were billeted at Montacute. Jim borrowed various items to display in the house, including some furniture from the basement of the Victoria & Albert Museum, 25 pictures from Haigh Hall near Wigan, and the books from Brockhampton Court in Herefordshire. The Long Gallery at Montacute is now used to display part of the National Portrait Gallery's collection.

1947 **Stourhead.** A Palladian mansion in Wiltshire which is famous today for its gardens. The house was donated by the

Hoare family, which had owned it for more than two hundred years. In 1902 much of the house was destroyed by fire, but it was rebuilt in the original style. Most of the contents had been saved from the fire, but the house was filled with far too much stuff when the National Trust acquired it. Jim and his colleagues spent a year sorting out the porcelain, books, paintings and sculptures. A third of the items were kept, a third went to other National Trust houses, and a third were sold to dealers.

1947 **Petworth**. A 17th-century house in Sussex with grounds landscaped by Capability Brown. The house had been in the Wyndham family for 250 years. It now houses a large collection of important art work including 19 paintings by Turner. The contents of the house were accepted by the nation in lieu of death duties. Lord Egremont and his family still live in part of the house. Jim spent two years persuading Lord Leconfield to hand over the house so that his heirs would be able to continue living there.

In September 1948 Jim went to Italy for a month with his friend Desmond Shawe-Taylor and had an audience with Pope Pius XII at Castel Gandolfo. He didn't enjoy the visit much because he was suffering from a bad cold. He didn't like the building and thought the medal he was given rather cheap, though he did find the experience of meeting the Pope moving and thought that he had an aura of calm and sanctity. By the end of 1950 Jim was exhausted and he gave up his job as Historic Buildings Secretary. He took a part-time job as Architectural Adviser to the National Trust, and also sat on various committees. In 1951 Jim's book *Tudor Renaissance* was published, the first new book on Tudor architecture for fifty years. While researching the book he had sometimes had to resort to guessing or to writing in general terms as he didn't have much to go on. Not much research on Tudor buildings had been done before. In the book he discusses how Henry

VIII embraced at first the Italian style of architectural decoration, then sent his Italian artists away after his break with Rome. Jim didn't approve of Italian classicism being dismissed. He found Tudor buildings uncivilised, and his Catholicism is on display throughout the book.

* * * * *

In November 1951, much to the surprise of all his friends who knew that he was gay, Jim married Alvilde Chaplin. He had met Alvilde in London in 1943, but did not fall in love with her until 1949. Born in 1909, Alvilde Bridges was the great-niece of Robert Bridges. She was apparently named after a Norwegian ballerina with whom her father had been having an affair. In 1933 Alvilde married Anthony Chaplin, who became the 3rd Viscount Chaplin, and they had a daughter, Clarissa, born in 1934. Anthony was a zoologist with not much money but many rich connections. The Chaplins moved in society and in 1937 they went to Paris so that Anthony could study music. There Alvilde met the Princesse de Polignac, known as Winnie, fell in love with her and went to live with her. The pair lived in Paris for two years, then moved to London when war broke out. Alvilde met lots of famous people from the art world at Winnie's Paris salons, including Cocteau, Colette and Gertrude Stein. Winnie also entertained French aristocrats such as the patrons of the arts Charles and Marie-Laure de Noailles.

Princess Winnaretta had been a society hostess in Paris for many years. She was the daughter of the American Isaac Singer who made his fortune from sewing machines, and the aunt of Daisy Fellowes whom she raised after the death of Daisy's mother. When Winnie was 29 she married for the second time. Her new husband was the 59 year old Prince Edmond de Polignac. Winnie was a confirmed lesbian and theirs was a lavender marriage, although they were united by their love of music and the arts. From 1923-33 Winnie had had an affair with Violet Trefusis. When Winnie died in 1943 she left Alvilde a house in France as well as a lot of money. Alvilde was already well off as her parents had died in the late 1930s and left her well provided for.

Jim first met Winnie and Alvilde in 1943 while attending the parties of Sibyl Colefax and Emerald Cunard. He was subsequently invited to some of Winnie's dinner parties in London and fell in love with Alvilde both for her beauty and her cooking ability. Anthony Chaplin was away serving in the RAF at this time. After the war Alvilde lived in her inherited house near Paris where she moved in French high society and also mixed with ex-patriots such as Nancy Mitford and Diana Cooper. In December 1948 Alvilde and Anthony took a house in London for a couple of months. Jim went to several dinner parties at their house, then he started taking just Alvilde to the theatre and to other dinner parties. In February 1949 he went on holiday to Rome with both Alvilde and Anthony. Alvilde and Jim went round the sights together while Anthony was busy studying Italian toads (he was keeping a rare one in a chamber pot in his hotel room). The three of them then drove to Florence, with Anthony stopping at ponds on the way to look at frogs and toads, and Jim and Alvilde stopping to look at buildings and art galleries. A week later Alvilde went to stay at the Dorchester for a week and Jim took her out every evening to dinner and the theatre. Jim and Anthony both spent Easter at Alvilde's house in France. During the rest of that year Jim and Alvilde spent much of their time together, some of it touring Provence and Italy and some of it in London. Both of them must have kept on good terms with Anthony, as in December Jim and Anthony had lunch together and discussed what to do. Anthony volunteered to get divorced, and Jim took Alvilde out that evening and told her he would marry her if she got divorced and got an annulment. The Chaplins divorced in 1950 and Anthony promptly married his mistress, Rosemary Lyttelton.

In January 1951 Jim took a part-time National Trust post as Historic Buildings Adviser. During that year he and Alvilde lived together in rented apartments in London. Alvilde sold her house near Paris and bought one in the south of France in a village near Monte Carlo. She had several friends living nearby, including Graham Sutherland, Somerset Maugham, and Prince Rainier. Jim and Alvilde married in November that year at a register office in London with Harold Nicolson and his wife Vita Sackville-West as witnesses, though the annulment of Alvilde's first marriage did not come through until several years later.

Alvilde was now a tax exile living in France, and Jim spent six months of each year living with her in the village of Roquebrune, and the other six months working for the National Trust. Alvilde joined him for three months each year in London, and they also travelled on the continent when he was researching his books on architecture. Alvilde was rich and shared the same cultural and social interests as Jim did. She was a wonderful cook and loved to entertain. She published several best-selling books on gardening and also designed gardens for distinguished people in France including the former French President Valery Giscard-d'Estaing and the pop star Mick Jagger. In 1955 Alvilde started a five-year affair with Vita Sackville-West. They shared an interest in gardening. They were very discreet, and only their close friends knew about it. Alvilde seems to have developed her passion for gardening due to Vita, and she later created wonderful gardens at her English homes Alderley Grange and Essex House. In 1980, together with Rosemary Verey, she edited *The Englishwoman's Garden* in which forty women wrote about their gardens, and in 1982 they edited *The Englishman's Garden*. Alvilde went on to write about interiors, publishing *The Englishman's House* in 1984 and *The Englishman's Room* in 1986, both with photographs by Derry

Moore.

* * * * *

From 1951 until 1958 Jim lived partly in London and partly in France. He also travelled a lot on the continent while researching his books on architecture. He and Alvilde often stayed in Venice and Florence, where they knew lots of members of the ex-patriot community. Jim spent winter in the Mediterranean, and then Alvilde lived with him in London from May to July each year. Lots of English friends would visit them in France, including Nancy Mitford, James Pope-Hennessy, Lennox Berkeley and Eddy Sackville-West. Other friends stayed in hotels or villas nearby. In 1953 Jim's book *The Age of Inigo Jones* was published. He had been inspired to write it on his first visit to Chatsworth in August 1948, when he saw a book of drawings by Inigo Jones. He liked the idea of writing about a self-taught amateur. The book got good reviews, including one by Harold Nicolson in *The Observer*. Another of Jim's books, *Roman Mornings*, was published in 1956. It contained eight essays about Jim's favourite monuments in Rome, and also some essays on aesthetics. He dedicated the book to Sachie Sitwell, who was also an architectural historian. It is an idiosyncratic selection of monuments – Jim finds the Trevi Fountain charming, but not of any architectural interest. He likes the church of Santa Maria di Cosmedin because it is very quiet and peaceful inside; you can't hear the roar of the traffic and he is the only visitor. Cyril Connolly reviewed the book in *The Sunday Times* and found it a difficult read, but rewarding. Despite mixed reviews the book was awarded the Heineman Prize.

* * * * *

Jim's next amorous adventure began in October 1958, when Harold Nicolson recommended someone he thought might be suitable for a new post which was coming up at the National Trust. John Kenworthy-Browne got the job, and he and Jim became close friends. Alvilde didn't approve of John, not least because he was only 27 and Jim was now 49. In January 1959 Jim visited Italy and took John with him as a research assistant. In February John stayed with Jim at his London home in Thursloe Square. Alvilde steamed open some letters from John which confirmed her suspicions, and Jim admitted that he was in love with him.

In April 1959 John went to live at Dyrham Park in Gloucestershire, a nearly derelict house which the National Trust had acquired in 1956. The Ministry of Works was busy restoring the building, and John was given a flat in it in which to live while he was the National Trust Representative for the Wessex and Severn Region. Dyrham Park opened to the public in June 1961. Alvilde was very jealous of Jim's relationship with John. Jim and John were very discreet, and only their close friends knew that they were an item. In October 1959 they visited Rome together. John left the National Trust in 1965 and went to work for Christie's in London, where Jim often stayed with him. It was between 1959 and 1961 that Jim researched and wrote *Earls of Creation*, which was published in 1962. It is a book about five 18th-century earls who loved architecture and landscape gardening. They were all fans of William Kent. They are: - Lord Bathurst of Cirencester Park, Lord Pembroke of Marble Hill House, Lord Burlington of Chiswick House, Lord Oxford of Wimpole Hall, and Lord Leicester of Holkham Hall. The book got good reviews and sold well.

* * * * *

Alvilde gave up her French house in 1959 and she and Jim spent much time in 1960 looking for a house in England as neither of them wanted to split up. Early in 1961 they finally found a house that they both liked. Alderley Grange was a Jacobean house in the Cotswolds which needed some work doing to it, and after having some repairs done they moved in in August. The house was only 20 minutes by car from Dyrham Park, so Jim was happy to live there. The garden was overgrown, but was gradually lovingly restored by Alvilde. It was at this time that Jim was asked by his friend John Betjeman to write *The Shell Guide to Worcestershire*. Betjeman was working at The Architectural Press and was the editor of the Shell Guides. He himself wrote the books on Devon and Cornwall, and he asked some of his friends to write books on other counties. Jim enjoyed travelling round Worcestershire and carrying out his research with his friend John Kenworthy-Browne. Jim did not hold back from saying exactly what he thought, and his rude remarks about the architecture of petrol stations had to be edited out of the book, as did some derogatory comments about Worcester Corporation wrecking the architecture of Worcester. The book was published in 1964.

In March 1966 Jim left the National Trust and became a full-time writer. He immediately started work on a book about the history of St. Peter's in Rome, travelling to the Vatican to discuss the project with the Pope's private secretary and to supervise the photography. The Pope asked for the book to be published in 1967, the supposed anniversary of St. Peter's martyrdom in AD 67. Jim already knew the building and its history well, and managed to complete the book by October 1966. He barely mentioned Vatican Two as he disapproved of mass in the vernacular and the use of contemporary liturgical music and modern art work. His friends Alan Pryce-Jones and Peter Quennell gave the book good reviews, but it didn't sell many copies.

Still concerned about what was happening in the Catholic church, in 1969 Jim drafted a letter to the Pope voicing his concern about changes to the Catholic ritual. He complained about the abandonment of Latin, which he thought meant that the Mass had lost its sense of mystery and become virtually indistinguishable from a protestant service. He also disapproved of what was happening in France where side chapels dedicated to individual saints were being broken up, statues removed, and incense being used less and less. It is not clear whether he actually sent the letter.

Jim was also becoming disillusioned with Catholicism for other reasons, including the Pope's refusal to endorse the use of contraception (Jim thought the world was becoming overpopulated). He blamed Catholicism for the situation in Northern Ireland, where he thought the Catholic Church was clandestinely encouraging the work of the IRA. And he no longer believed in transubstantiation. He liked the Anglican church at Alderley where he lived, and he liked the vicar. Alvilde was an Anglican, and he started attending the parish church with her and participating in village life. There was no specific date on which he stopped being a catholic. He still attended some catholic services when in London, including at least one at Brompton Oratory in 1972, but in 1973 he became a church warden at Alderley and in March 1974 he wrote to *The Times* complaining about the Pope's attitude to birth control.

Throughout the 1970s Jim continued to write, and in 1970 *Another Self* was published. This is a book of memoirs recounting some of the more hilarious incidents in his life, not all of which appear to be true. From 1970-73, while still a Catholic, Jim was researching a book about the Catholic Stuarts in exile. He carried out research in the Vatican library and also visited Scotland to see places associated with Bonnie Prince Charlie and to research the prince's estranged wife and his younger brother. The book was rejected for publication and he put it to one side, hoping that it might be published later. In 1981 Chatto's agreed to publication. Jim rewrote parts of the book as by then he had access to the Royal Archives at Windsor, and it was published in 1983 under the title *The Last Stuarts*.

Unlike Jim, his old friend Nancy Mitford was not faring too well by the early 1970s. She had been suffering from Hodgkin's disease since 1968 and was in a lot of pain. In September 1972 Alvilde arranged for her to move into a nursing home in London. When Jim visited her there in January 1973 she was rather deaf and had difficulty hearing what he was saying, though she was pleased to see him. She told him that she read all day. They had exchanged letters ever since the war and he was impressed that she could write such jolly missives when she was in such pain. After Nancy's death in June 1973 Jim continued his friendship with her sisters Pam, Diana and Deborah. He often went to stay at Chatsworth House, which he had been visiting ever since Deborah and her husband Andrew had moved in in 1959. Pam and Diana sometimes stayed there at the same time. Occasionally Alvilde would accompany him. He visited Diana in France at least once a year, renewing his friendship and correspondence to such an extent that she came to regard him as her oldest friend.

* * * * *

In 1975 the Lees-Milnes sold their house, Alderley Grange, apparently after deciding that the house was too large for them and the upkeep too expensive. They moved to a flat in Lansdown Crescent, Bath, where Jim's hero William Beckford had had his library. But they soon decided that both the flat and the garden were too small, and at the end of 1975 they moved to Essex House, a rented 17th-century house on the Badminton Estate with an acre of garden. They kept the flat in Bath, which was only a 30-mile drive from Badminton, and Jim worked there every day on his biography of Beckford.

William Beckford was an art collector, critic and travel writer. He was also a member of parliament and the builder of Fonthill Abbey and Lansdown Tower (known as Beckford's Tower). The tower is a folly in neo-classical style on the top of Lansdown Hill in Bath, and was built in 1827. It is 120 feet tall. When Beckford was short of money in 1822 he sold Fonthill and some of its contents and moved the rest of the contents to the crescent and the tower. The contents of the abbey included books, paintings, prints, Asian objets d'art, French furniture and statues. The tower was restored in 1995 and is now a museum. It is owned by the Bath Preservation Trust and is Grade I listed. Jim's life of Beckford, entitled simply *William Beckford*, was published in 1976.

From 1976-81 Jim worked on his two-volume biography of Harold Nicolson. After Vita's death in 1962 Harold lived at Sissinghurst on his own and went into a decline. He died in 1968. In 1976 Nigel Nicolson, Harold's son, asked Jim to write Harold's biography. Jim was reluctant at first as he knew little about diplomacy and politics and wasn't interested in them. Eventually he agreed because Nigel and his brother Ben were both so keen for him to do it. The book took him five years to write because there was such a huge amount of material. The material included diaries, letters, thousands of diplomatic dispatches, hundreds of parliamentary speeches recorded in Hansard, and thirty books. Jim also interviewed lots of people who had known Harold. The book was awarded the Royal Society of Literature's Heineman Prize, but did not sell very well.

Jim went on to write four more books between 1982 and 1988. *Images of Bath* was published by Bamber Gascoigne in 1982. Bamber provided the American photographer David Ford to help Jim with the book. Jim's next book, *The Enigmatic Edwardian* ,was published in 1986. It is a biography of Reginald, 2nd Viscount Esher. Esher's grandson, Lionel, met Jim at a concert in 1982 and asked him to write the book. Jim considered himself a strange choice, as he had fallen out with Esher more than ten years previously over the redevelopment of Bath. It transpired that Lionel had already asked three other people to write the biography, but they had turned it down. Jim had to go to Churchill College, Cambridge to look through Esher's papers, and was appalled to find that it resembled a giant public lavatory. He thought that Churchill would have hated the building even more than he hated the portrait of him by Graham Sutherland. The book was eventually published after Lionel had persuaded Jim to remove some references to Esher's homosexuality.

Jim's first book on architecture for some time, *Some Cotswold Country Houses,* was published in 1987. He had previously lost interest in the National Trust and architecture after deciding that the battle for conservation was lost. David Burnett of the Dovecote Press asked him to write the book, and volunteered to drive him round the houses. They visited the houses in March and April 1987, and found that the houses which were still lived in by descendants of the people who had built them were on the whole well maintained, but that some of the lesser houses had been bought by rich commuters and done up in what Jim considered to be bad taste. He was also shocked at the state of some large houses which had been bought by developers, but didn't mind too much the idea of some of them being converted into flats. Jim's next book, *Venetian Evenings,* was published in 1988. The book involved him spending ten days on his own in Venice making his choice of monuments and studying them. He discovered that he had gone off Venice as it was now full of noisy teenagers and litter.

* * * * *

Jim's next project lasted from 1988-91 and involved him researching and writing a book about the 6th Duke of Devonshire which Deborah Devonshire (nee Mitford) had asked him to write. The Duke was an art collector and patron of Joseph Paxton, and Jim's research involved lots of visits to the Devonshires' homes Chatsworth House, Lismore Castle and Bolton Abbey. The book, *The Bachelor Duke*, was published in 1991. The following year *People and Places,* which is about Jim's part in procuring various houses for the National Trust, was published.

In November 1992 Jim was offered the CBE in recognition of his conservation work, but he turned it down. He didn't want the bother because he was too old. Receiving the award would have involved investiture, fuss, and dinner. 1992 had been a difficult year for Jim, with much of it spent caring for Alvilde. She had had heart trouble since 1990, when she had an operation to replace a faulty heart valve. In March 1992 she collapsed and fell into a coma but gradually recovered, though she was left having to walk with sticks. She gradually became frailer, and on 18 March 1994 Jim got home from his day in Bath (where he still went every day to work on his writing in Beckford's library) to find her lying on the garden path, dead. She had slipped on the path, fallen, and suffered a heart attack. Jim missed her dreadfully, but her death meant he was able to go out and about a lot. During the next couple of years he visited Chatsworth, Venice, Scotland, and various friends in various parts of England. It was during this period that he wrote his last book, which is a series of memoirs about friends he had known over the years. The friends about whom Jim writes include Vita Sackville-West, Rosamond Lehmann, Sacheverell Sitwell, Osbert Lancaster, Robert Byron, James Pope-Hennessy and John Fowler. *Fourteen Friends* was published in 1996.

Jim had been in poor health for some time and in August 1997 he went into hospital for a major cancer operation. He had first been diagnosed with cancer in 1984 and had had several operations since then. In September he was discharged from hospital and kept up a busy social life. On 4th November he travelled to Paris with Debo Devonshire to visit Diana Mosley. He fell ill on the 5th and returned to England on the 6th. He was taken to the Royal United Hospital in Bath, then at the end of November he moved to Tetbury Cottage Hospital where he died on 28th December.

CHAPTER FOUR – PETER WATSON

Peter Watson (1908-1956) was a wealthy art collector and patron of the arts. He was educated at Eton and St John's College, Oxford. He funded the literary magazine *Horizon* and was also instrumental in setting up the Institute of Contemporary Arts.

* * * * *

Victor William Peter Watson (known as Peter) was born on 14 September 1908. His mother Bessie was the daughter of the manager of a steelworks in Cumberland and was brought up in Workington. Peter's father, Sir George Watson, made his fortune selling margarine before World War One. In 1887 he set up the Maypole Dairy Company which sold butter, margarine and cheese, and by 1914 he had 1,000 shops. In 1910 Sir George was able to buy a large country estate on the River Thames at Sulhamstead Abbots near Reading, and in 1912 he became a baronet. Peter had an elder brother and sister who were both a lot older than he was. His brother, Sir Norman Watson, was in the Royal Air Force during World War One. He had joined straight from Eton and never went to university. In 1934 he formed the Heston Aircraft Company, becoming its chairman. He went on to build a ski resort in Canada. Peter's sister, Florence, became a county lady who liked dogs and horses. She trained and bred racehorses and campaigned for women to be allowed to become jockeys. She married in 1916 and left home when Peter was eight.

In 1921 Peter went up to Eton, where he was embarrassed that the family fortune came from margarine. He disliked school because a lot of the other boys were snobbish about people who were in trade. Peter was neither good at sport nor an intellectual, but luckily for him he was in Goodhart's house, and Arthur Goodhart was very laid back – he did not care whether or not the house won any cups. Peter made friends with a boy called Alan Pryce-Jones, who was in the same division (form) but in Whitworth House. Alan remembers Peter as being terribly sophisticated, rich, and very funny. Other Eton contemporaries included James Lees-Milne, George Orwell, Anthony Powell, Ian Fleming and Hamish Erskine. Peter left Eton at Christmas 1926 without having made his mark in any way.

* * * * *

In 1927 Peter went up to St John's College, Oxford to read Modern Languages, but later changed to Politics, Philosophy and Economics (PPE). His friend Alan Pryce-Jones, who would go on to be editor of the *Times Literary Supplement* from 1948-59, was at Magdalen College. Peter started his student days as a very frivolous person. In his second year he shared rooms with Nancy Mitford's friend Hamish Erskine, and they gave lavish luncheon parties and cocktail parties for their fellow undergraduates. Hamish and Peter, together with other students, would frequent the Mitford family home at weekends and annoy Nancy's father with their frivolous ways. Once when Peter rang to speak to Nancy and her father answered the 'phone she was told that 'that hog Watson' was on the line, and thereafter Nancy's nickname for Peter became 'Hog'.

Peter later became friendly with W H Auden and Stephen Spender. By 1929 Auden, Spender and their friend Christopher Isherwood were living in Germany, and Peter joined them there when he spent some time at a language school trying to improve his German. He enjoyed visiting the night clubs, where his friends introduced him to some attractive working-class German boys. His German was still not up to scratch, however, and in January 1930 he was sent down from Oxford after just over two years, having failed several exams during that time.

When Peter was 22 he inherited a trust fund of one million pounds which made him one of the richest men in Britain. Unlike most other men with a similar income he had no house, estate or family to support, so there was no need for him to have a career or even look for a job of any sort. In November 1930, much to Nancy Mitford's amusement he bought himself (according to her description) a coral-coloured Rolls Royce with inlaid gems and fur-covered seats. He became for a time the boyfriend of the theatre designer Oliver Messel, with whom he travelled on the Continent in 1930. On a visit to Vienna to look for antiques they met Cecil Beaton, who was already becoming well known as a photographer. Cecil, who was a social climber and consequently not universally popular, (Jean Cocteau referred to him as Malice in Wonderland) fell in love with Peter. They travelled in Europe together, but Cecil's love was not reciprocated and Peter indulged himself with boys he met in places such as Paris and Munich. Peter was fond of Cecil but not attracted to him either physically or intellectually. When Cecil went to America to do some work for the magazine *Vogue*, Peter went with him. They visited the Caribbean together but never became lovers, although they remained friends on and off. In London Cecil introduced Peter to art and art galleries, and Peter taught Cecil about music. Peter was also a guest at house parties at Ashcombe, Cecil's country house in Wiltshire.

During the first half of the 1930s Peter travelled extensively, mainly in Germany and Austria. He was one of the first people to actually acknowledge that they liked the work of the Modernist painters and sculptors. He used some of his wealth to purchase items by people such as Picasso,

Braque, Miro, Dali, Giacometti and Ernst. Peter himself sat for a portrait by the Russian émigré artist Pavel Tchelitchew, who at that stage of his life was painting in the Neo-Romantic style. This style did not really interest Peter – he had only agreed to the portrait because Cecil Beaton had asked for it. In Paris Peter stayed with the well-known society hostess and patron of the arts Marie-Laure de Noailles. She and her husband Charles had sponsored the work of Cocteau and Dali, and also commissioned Poulenc to write music to be performed at two of their balls. Marie-Laure introduced Peter to her friends in the art and music worlds, and he became increasingly interested in art and less and less enamoured with the world of the Bright Young Things which he had left behind in London.

In January 1935 Peter visited Austria and Switzerland and then went on to Munich. He liked Germany because of the delightful young men he encountered in the bars and nightclubs, but he had also developed an interest in German Renaissance art and may have been hoping to purchase some pictures for his collection. While he was sitting in a café with a young man, Peter was arrested and apparently accused of currency violations. He was told by the police to go and wait in his hotel, but as he was worried that his arrest might have something to do with his homosexuality he took a train to Austria instead. Due to the developing political situation Germany was becoming an unsafe place for people such as Peter. He would make two more brief visits to that country later in the year, but after being detained by the border police for two days on one of those trips he never went to Nazi Germany again.

Back in London Peter had been visited by Marie-Laure de Noailles, a visit which led to his first act of sponsorship of the arts. Marie-Laure was looking for backing for Diaghilev's protégé, the Ukrainian-born conductor and composer Igor Markevitch. Markevitch had written an oratorio *Le Paradis Perdu* based on Milton's *Paradise Lost* which was originally meant to premiere in Brussels but had run out of time for rehearsals. Peter went to Paris to meet Markevitch, and agreed to try and arrange for the BBC to host a performance. The summer of 1935 found Peter touring Switzerland and Italy, then in September he travelled on to Greece with Markevitch. The latter's *Le Paradis Perdu* was eventually broadcast live by the BBC from the concert hall at Broadcasting House on 20th December 1935. It had mixed reviews, but went on to be performed in Brussels and Paris in the spring of 1936.

By 1936 Peter had decided that Paris was the centre of the arts, and that that was where he wanted to live with his new lover. Peter had first met Denham Fouts, who was basically an American prostitute (Truman Capote, with whom Denham later had a fling, described him as 'The best-kept boy in the world'), in Berlin in 1933 when they had a one-night stand. After that the pair didn't meet for several years, though they wrote to each other from time to time. During those intervening years Denham was the lover of Evan Morgan (second Viscount Tredegar) and of Prince Paul of Greece. In August 1936 Denham had gone to The United States to visit his family, and in December Peter crossed the Atlantic to track him down. They returned to London and settled in Peter's home there, but by the middle of 1937 were touring Europe together. Peter moved on to Paris, staying in a series of hotels including The Ritz whilst he was looking for a suitable apartment in which to house his art collection and his lover. In the interim he enjoyed Parisian cultural life, attending plays and ballets and the international exhibition at which Picasso's *Guernica* was first seen by the general public. Peter himself bought one of Picasso's other paintings, the 1934 work *Girl Reading* which was a portrait of Picasso's lover Marie-Therese Walter.

By October Peter had failed to find an apartment which met all his needs, and he decided to take Denham on a trip to the Far East in order to avoid the cold of a European winter. Travelling via the Mediterranean, Suez and Singapore, they reached Shanghai when it had just fallen to the Japanese after four months of intense fighting. Shanghai night life, however, was still thriving despite the devastation, and a bar on the waterfront turned out to belong to an old German friend of Peter's from Berlin. In view of the deteriorating situation Peter decided to go on to America via Hong Kong. Denham, who had a penchant for Chinese youths and apparently hoped to get a job in the friend's bar, stayed in Shanghai.

From Hong Kong Peter went on to Hawaii, Los Angeles and New York, meeting up with various old friends including Tchelitchew, who had moved to America in 1934. In New York it was arranged that Peter would provide financial backing for Tchelitchew's boyfriend, Charley Ford, who had just written a book of poetry called The Garden of Disorder. The book was published later that year. By May 1938 Peter was back in England and from there he went on to Marseilles to meet up with Denham, who had tired of life in Shanghai.

In the summer of 1938 Peter finally found an apartment which met his needs to rent in Paris. After he and Denham had moved in he spent several months searching for suitable paintings to adorn the walls and purchased works by artists including Braque, Klee, Miro and Dali. He sold his house in London and also sold off some of the paintings which had been on display there. Some of the other art works from the London house went into storage, and others were sent to Peter's mother's home. Peter's Parisian flat soon became a haven for ex-pats, and he had visits from Cyril Connolly and his wife Jean, Stephen Spender, Brian Howard and W H Auden among others. Peter and Denham also became friendly with Gertrude Stein and her lover Alice B Toklas, who had stayed on in Paris when most of the other Americans had been scared away by the threat of war.

In the summer of 1939 Peter and his friend Stephen

Spender went on a tour of Switzerland, visiting Paul Klee who had been living in Berne since fleeing Germany in 1933 (Klee's work was considered very degenerate by the Nazis). They also met up with other art dealers and patrons of the arts, including Christophe Bernoulli who lived in Basle.

* * * * *

When World War Two broke out Peter was in Paris and Denham was on a fishing holiday in Finland. Somehow Denham managed to get back to London through occupied Europe. Peter sent him to America where he thought he would be safe, giving him Picasso's *Girl Reading* to take to New York for an exhibition there. Denham, who said he was a conscientious objector, spent most of the war in California living off Peter's money. He had a long affair with Christopher Isherwood, who wrote a novel called *Down There On A Visit* about his relationship with Denham. In December 1945 Denham sold *Girl Reading* for 12,500 dollars in order to pay off his debts. During his relationship with Denham Peter had tried to sort out Denham's opium addiction, but he must have realised eventually that Denham was just using him and wanted his money. Later Denham became the lover of Truman Capote, who based some of the characters in his novels on him. Eventually he went to Rome with a new lover, and died of a drug overdose in 1948. It turned out that he also had a serious heart condition.

But to return to our sheep. Peter moved back to London when war broke out in 1939 and took a job in the offices of the Red Cross. He found himself working with Eddy Sackville-West, who shared his love of modern music and had been working as music critic at the *New Statesman*. Eddy had been promoting the work of British composers such as Benjamin

Britten and Michael Tippett, and Peter became a friend and patron of Tippett. Peter was called up in late 1941 and applied to join the RAF, but he was rejected on health grounds because he was so thin. Back in London he worked in Zwemmer's book shop and gallery in Charing Cross Road and began collecting art all over again. During the blitz he never went to air raid shelters, saying that he would rather die in his sleep. He was impressed by the way Londoners dealt with the hardships of the blitz. His flat in Palace Gate became a haven for his friends, who could borrow his books of Kafka, Rimbaud and Baudelaire, or listen to his records of Stravinsky and Berg. He also had copies of French literary magazines. In the early 1940s, having visited St Ives a couple of times, Peter became interested in contemporary British art. He also went to St David's and encouraged his artist friends to go there because of the light. The Graham Sutherlands were already living in the area, and Peter encouraged John Craxton to paint there. In 1944 Craxton had his first solo exhibition at the Leicester Galleries in London. This time round Peter collected mostly English art, including works by Graham Sutherland, John Piper, John Minton and John Craxton. Later in 1944 Peter moved to a house in the Sussex countryside which he rented for a year from the painter Dick Wyndham. Peter and Cyril Connolly had previously been to parties there in the 1930s, and Cyril had described the house in his book *The Unquiet Grave.* Peter put Dick's old-fashioned furniture in store and replaced it with modern stuff. He invited his London friends to dinner, offering good produce from local farms which was not available in the capital. He still kept his flat in London and visited it occasionally, but flying bombs were hitting London by then and it was prudent to remain in the countryside.

* * * * *

In 1940 Peter and his friend Cyril Connolly (whom Peter had known since meeting him in Austria in 1937) had founded the literary magazine *Horizon*, which would be published for a decade. Peter funded the magazine throughout its life. He was its art editor from 1940-49, and he himself wrote articles on people such as Joan Miro and translated a lot of contributions from the original French and Italian. The magazine was edited by Cyril and briefly co-edited by Stephen Spender. It was supposed to contribute to the war effort by boosting morale, and it aimed to uphold western art and civilisation (Nancy Mitford thought that Peter and Cyril were avoiding military service by founding a magazine, though editing a magazine wasn't a reserved occupation. She didn't approve of lefties not serving, was anti-fascist and thought all men should fight, like her husband who was in the Welsh Guards). The magazine called itself 'A Review of Literature and Art', and would eventually come to be regarded as the best literary magazine in the English-speaking world. The magazine aimed to be apolitical. Auden and Isherwood had gone to America and the left-wing era was coming to a close. The literary experiment which had combined Marxism and Modernism was ending.

Prominent writers who contributed to *Horizon* over the years include Graham Greene, Bertrand Russell, Virginia Woolf, Vita Sackville-West, John Betjeman, Dylan Thomas, T S Eliot and Edith Sitwell. Artists whose work was featured include John Craxton, Robert Colquhoun, John Minton, John Piper, Graham Sutherland, Lucian Freud, Augustus John and Paul Klee. Work by emerging writers was also published in *Horizon*. Some of George Orwell's earliest work, which included essays on politics and popular culture, was included (George Orwell had been a friend of Cyril Connolly's since their Eton days). In August 1941 Orwell wrote an article attacking H G Wells – Orwell didn't like him advocating a 'peaceful world state' and thought that everyone ought to fight. Another important writer, the Hungarian-born Arthur Koestler, had just arrived in London as a refugee. Cyril Connolly recognised his potential and published three important articles by him between 1942 and 1944. In 1947

Angus Wilson had been unable to find a publisher for his short stories and was working at the British Museum. The publication of two of his stories in *Horizon* no doubt brought him to the attention of the literary world, and his first book of stories, *The Wrong Set*, was published in 1949. During the second half of the 1940s *Horizon* began publishing books through Chatto & Windus. These included books on art but also works by people such as Sartre, Gide, Philip Toynbee and e e cummings, and Cyril Connolly's own novel, *The Unquiet Grave*. Evelyn Waugh's novella, *The Loved One*, took up an entire issue of *Horizon*. In Evelyn Waugh's novel *Unconditional Surrender,* the third book in the *Sword of Honour* trilogy, *Horizon* is satirised as *Survival*, and Cyril Connolly is satirised as Everard Spruce. Everard edits a literary magazine, likes good food and parties, and is always surrounded by young ladies. After the war *Horizon* broadened its scope and began to cover modern French writing extensively. Cyril soon realised that what was coming out of Paris was new and important, and there were lots of articles by or about Sartre, Camus, Gide and de Beauvoir. He also took an interest in American art and literature, and the magazine included an article on Jackson Pollock, essays on American culture, and poems by e e cummings and W H Auden (Auden had become a US citizen in 1946). But by the end of 1949 Cyril had to acknowledge that most new writing was now coming out of America, and *Horizon* was becoming very expensive to produce. Cyril himself wanted to concentrate on his own writing rather than editing a magazine, and *Horizon* closed in January 1950 after 102 issues.

* * * * *

When the war broke out Peter had had to leave his art collection behind in Paris. He left some of his paintings by people such as Klee, Ernst, Picasso and Dali in his apartment, and other works were put in storage. He left his apartment in the care of the Romanian art critic Sherban Sidery, which proved to be a big mistake. Peter's pictures seem to have been appropriated by the SS and sold off, though after the war he found several of them in art galleries belonging to people who had been his friends. In late 1944 or early 1945 the art historian Douglas Cooper discovered some paintings which had belonged to Peter stored at the Jeu de Paume. They had been rescued in August 1944 from a train which was on its way to Germany with looted art works. In July 1945 Peter and Cyril Connolly managed to get to Paris on *Horizon* business – they were looking for people to write articles for the magazine. Peter got back to his flat, but the paintings and most of the furniture had gone, and the flat was very dirty. The pair only stayed in Paris for a week and then went on to Switzerland. Cyril, ever the opportunist, thought that there might be some decent food in a country which hadn't been involved in the war. In a gallery in Basle Peter saw one of his own Dali's from his Paris apartment on display. He discovered that the painting had passed through several hands, starting with friends and going on to a museum in Zurich and thence to Basle. A couple of years later in Paris he saw another of the paintings which he had owned in the window of an art gallery. In Switzerland Peter and Cyril started arguing and fell out. Peter developed jaundice and spent two months in a Swiss clinic, while Cyril abandoned him in callous fashion and returned to England.

When Peter had recovered he started travelling round America and Europe again, but due to currency restrictions he couldn't do it in as much style as he used to. He discovered that, like Kenneth Clark and Colin Anderson, he found the new post-war art styles of Abstraction and Expressionism distasteful. He thought that the war had been fought in defence of what he regarded as Civilisation, and felt depressed at the state of things. In 1939 he had supported Auden and

Isherwood but now he was disgusted that they, along with Dali and his wife, had spent the war in California (although he was reconciled with all of them later on). Peter turned to supporting British art and artists and provided financial assistance to Francis Bacon, Lucian Freud and John Craxton. In 1947 he was the main benefactor when the Institute of Contemporary Arts (ICA), which was planned as the British equivalent of New York's Museum of Modern Art, was founded in London. Other co-founders were Roland Penrose and Herbert Read. Peter saw the ICA as a way of educating the public in modern art, and he put on exhibitions by people such as Freud and Bacon. He was heavily involved in the running of the ICA, attending lots of committee meetings, arranging exhibitions, and helping with hangings. The ICA's first exhibition, which was held in 1948, was called 'Forty Years of Modern Art' and featured work by British artists such as Bacon, Craxton, Freud and Colquhoun. Overseas contributors included Magritte, Matisse. Mondrian, Picasso and Miro. The ICA also put on poetry readings by people such as T S Eliot, Dylan Thomas, Cecil Day Lewis and W H Auden.

In 1950 the ICA moved to permanent premises in Mayfair and Peter himself chose all the paintings for the first exhibition there, which was entitled '1950: Aspects of British Art'. Putting his wealth to good use, he personally sponsored some of the work of artists in the 1940s and 1950s. He also paid the rent on several studios so that artists such as Freud and Craxton could work in London. In 1955 Peter was involved in the organisation of a Francis Bacon exhibition at the ICA. He wrote letters to all his contacts asking them to lend their paintings. The choice of pictures to be displayed was made jointly between Peter and Bacon and ranged from a pastel done in 1930 to oils painted in 1954. Paintings were leant by, amongst others, Sir Colin Anderson, the British Council, Lucian Freud and the Hanover Gallery. There were also loans from various private collectors.

* * * * *

By the 1950s Peter had become a very different person from the one he was before the war. He was no longer elegant or ostentatiously rich, and sometimes went about unshaven and without a tie. He started voting Labour and gave up his large car and his luxurious way of life, though he did later run a smaller car. By 1956 he felt depressed and sick. The world had changed, and it seems as though he no longer wanted to be a part of it. He was living in Rutland Gate, Knightsbridge with his current lover, the American Norman Fowler, and had written a will which made Fowler his heir. On 3rd May 1956 Peter was found dead in his bath, with the door locked and the tap still running. Some people said that he was murdered by Fowler, although the coroner's verdict was 'accidental death'. Fowler rapidly sold all Peter's art works and books and pocketed the money. He moved to the Caribbean and set up a shark-hunting business with his new-found wealth. After that failed he spent his time doing jigsaw puzzles until he drowned in his bath at the age of 44.

CHAPTER FIVE – EVELYN WAUGH

Evelyn Waugh (1903-1966) was a novelist and travel writer. He is best remembered today for his novel *Brideshead Revisited* but he also wrote satirical novels about the lives of the Bright Young Things, travel books about Africa and South America, and biographies.

* * * * *

Arthur Evelyn St John Waugh (known as Evelyn) was born in Hampstead on October 28th 1903. His father, Arthur Waugh, was managing director of the publishing firm Chapman & Hall. He was a distant figure, and their relationship would become the basis for that between Charles Ryder and his father in Evelyn's magnum opus, *Brideshead Revisited*. Evelyn was initially taught at home by his mother, Catherine, then went as a day pupil to Heath Mount Preparatory School where he spent six happy years. He was a bully, and many years later Cecil Beaton still recalled being bullied by him. Outside school Evelyn wrote plays and got the neighbouring children to perform in them. During World War One he organised a group of boys who built a fort, paraded, and went on manoeuvres. It had been planned that Evelyn would go to Sherborne School, but due to a scandal involving his elder brother Alec, who had been expelled after a homosexual incident, Evelyn was sent to what he considered an inferior establishment, Lancing College.

Evelyn went up to Lancing in May 1917 and soon settled in. He became interested in art and November of that year saw his first published article, 'In Defence of Cubism', which was featured in the school's arts magazine. In drawing classes he learnt calligraphy and decorative design, and the skills which he acquired at Sherborne later led to him being asked to design book jackets for Chapman & Hall. Evelyn was also interested in literature and set up the 'Dilettanti Society' which was designed to promote art and literature and to foster political debate. One of the boys who joined the society was Tom Driberg, the future gossip columnist and member of parliament who would later be described as 'The Soul of Indiscretion'. Evelyn's cynicism was evident even at this early stage in his life, as evinced by his ridiculing of the school's cadet corps and setting up of 'The Corpse Club' for those who were weary of life. Later in his school career he became much more conventional and was house captain, editor of the school magazine and president of the debating society. He left Lancing in December 1921 with a scholarship to read Modern History at Hertford College, Oxford.

Evelyn went up to Oxford in January 1922. His first two terms, rather like those of Charles Ryder in *Brideshead*, were rather uneventful, though he did contribute some caricatures done in the wood-cut style to *Isis*, one of the undergraduate magazines. Later he contributed some drawings of modern versions of The Seven Deadly Sins to the *Cherwell*, the other main student publication. The sins had titles such as 'The Horrid Sacrilege of those that Ill-Treat Books' and 'That Dull Old Sin, Adultery'. At this stage Evelyn seems to have been thinking of making his living as an illustrator rather than an author. Then in the autumn of that year he met a young man called Harold Acton, became part of the Acton set, and all thoughts of studying for a degree went out of the window. Evelyn first met Harold when he went to hear G K Chesterton giving a talk at a meeting of the Newman Society, although he himself was not yet a Catholic. Terence Greenidge, who was a second year undergraduate at Hertford College, introduced Evelyn to the Hypocrites Club, Evelyn took Harold along to it, and the club was soon transformed from a sedate place where students met to drink beer and discuss philosophy into an establishment renowned for its drunkenness and fancy dress parties. Wealthy students such as Harold Acton, Gavin Henderson and Bryan Guinness also gave lavish luncheon parties which went on all afternoon in their rooms. Evelyn was soon being invited to these parties and got to know some of their rich Old Etonian friends. Harold's grand rooms in Christ Church were to become the model for Sebastian's rooms in Evelyn's novel *Brideshead Revisited,* and Harold's friend Hugh Lygon would become the model for Sebastian himself. Evelyn soon acquired a taste for the high life lived by his wealthy friends, and he ran up large bills with his tailor and other tradesmen in his efforts to keep up with the set to which he now belonged. Life after university became a distant prospect too gloomy to contemplate. Evelyn's distaste for studying was not helped by his loathing of his history tutor, the Dean of Hertford Charles Cruttwell, whose name would later be used for several unsavoury characters in Evelyn's novels.

Evelyn's time at Oxford was not entirely dissipated, however. Harold Acton had co-founded and edited a magazine called *The Oxford Broom* which was designed to sweep old traditions out of Oxford. For the June 1923 issue Evelyn wrote a short story called 'Antony, Who Sought Things That Were Lost'. In the story the Lady Elizabeth's lover, Count Antony, has been imprisoned, and she begs to be incarcerated with him because she can't bear the separation. Evelyn also designed the covers for each issue of *The Oxford Broom.* In his final year at Oxford he became sub-editor of *Isis* magazine, for which he wrote film reviews with comments such 'I don't think I have ever been bored quite so much' and 'Sheer, over-acted, senseless sentiment'.

In June 1924 Evelyn left Oxford without a degree, although he had managed to do sufficient work at the last moment to qualify for a third. In order to gain a degree in those days it was necessary to have been resident in Oxford for nine terms, and Evelyn's father considered it a waste of money to support his son in one more term of debauchery. Evelyn was therefore forced to do something about earning his living.

* * * * *

In September 1924, still thinking he might be able to earn his living as an illustrator, Evelyn started a course at an art school in London and went back to living with his parents. Most weekends were spent back in Oxford, visiting old friends and partying. By Christmas he had decided that he was not suited to the art course and was busy applying for teaching jobs at preparatory schools, a common stop-gap for those who had recently left university. He managed to get one at a school in North Wales; the only question he recalled being asked at the interview was whether he possessed a dinner jacket, such a garment being needed in order to impress the boys' parents. Evelyn started at the school in January 1925, taking with him the manuscript of a novel he was working on, *The Temple At Thatch*. He did not enjoy teaching, and after two terms handed in his notice when his brother Alec arranged a job for him in Italy as secretary to a translator. Unfortunately the job fell through, Harold Acton's comments on *The Temple At Thatch* were so scathing that Evelyn decided to burn the manuscript, and his half-hearted attempt at suicide by drowning was only prevented when he was stung by jellyfish and recovered his senses. One good thing did happen to Evelyn in 1925 however. In May he had written a short story called *The Balance*, which was an experiment in Modernist writing, and in 1926 this was included by Chapman & Hall in an anthology called *Georgian Stories*. This was Evelyn's first commercially published work.

By September 1925 Evelyn had managed to acquire a post at a school in Aston Clinton, Buckinghamshire, which he found much more congenial. There were two added attractions – his old Oxford friend Richard Plunket-Greene was already teaching there, and the school was within relatively easy reach of both Oxford and London. Evelyn promptly bought a motorbike on which to reach both cities, and the job lasted until he was dismissed after apparently making drunken overtures to a school matron. In the summer of 1926 Evelyn wrote an extended essay on the Pre-Raphaelite Brotherhood in the style of Lytton Strachey and had it privately printed by his old university friend Alastair Graham, who was training as a printer. This essay led to a contract from an old Oxford friend, Anthony Powell of the publishing firm Duckworth, to write a biography of Rossetti, and was in effect the beginning of Evelyn's literary career.

The biography was swiftly and easily written, and by September 1927 Evelyn was wondering what to do next in order to raise some money and to relieve the tedium of living with his parents in Hampstead. He hit on the idea of writing a comic novel based on his experiences as a preparatory school teacher, and the result was his first novel *Decline and Fall,* which was published by his father's firm in 1928. The book describes the antics of Paul Pennyfeather, who has been sent down from Oxford and has to take a teaching job at an obscure school. Paul is attracted to the wealthy mother of one of his pupils and becomes engaged to her, but on the morning of the wedding he is arrested and sentenced to seven years in prison. The book received very favourable reviews, including one from *The Guardian* praising Evelyn's ability to write dialogue, and another by Arnold Bennett in *The Evening Standard* describing it as a 'brilliantly malicious satire'.

* * * * *

By the mid 1920s the parties of the Bright Young Things were in full swing. Several friends from Evelyn's Oxford days were now settled in London, and he attended many parties with them. The parties were often fancy dress, and included bathing parties, circus parties, Wild West parties, a Mozart party, a second childhood party, parties where you dressed as someone you knew, parties where you dressed as someone famous etc etc. Sometimes Evelyn would just sit on a sofa observing everyone, taking in the ambience and subconsciously amassing material for his next novel, *Vile Bodies*. Tom Driberg, Evelyn's friend from his Lancing days, attended the parties as part of his job as gossip columnist for the *Daily Express*. Some of the parties took place at the London home of Bryan Guinness, an old university friend of Evelyn's who by now was married to Diana Mitford, one of Nancy's younger sisters.

It was during the party season of 1927 that Evelyn met and became attracted to Evelyn Gardner (their friends immediately started referring to them as He-Evelyn and She-Evelyn to avoid confusion). They became engaged in December of that year, much to the chagrin of Lady Burghclere, She-Evelyn's mother. Lady Burghclere did not want her daughter to marry someone with no regular source of income, but after the success of *Decline and Fall* Evelyn had sufficient money to support a wife and the two Evelyns married in June 1928. It was a private, hurriedly arranged wedding with Harold Acton acting as best man and another Oxford friend, Robert Byron, giving the bride away. Many people opined that She-Evelyn was only marrying in order to avoid having to go back and live with her mother, and this may indeed have been the case. As a result of the success of *Decline and Fall* He-Evelyn was commissioned by Duckworth to write a travel book, and in February 1929 the Waughs set off on an expenses-paid Mediterranean cruise which they treated as a delayed honeymoon. She-Evelyn's health had not been good; she had recently suffered from both influenza and German measles, and on the cruise she developed double pneumonia. He-Evelyn was obliged to engage a nurse to look after her, and by the time the ship reached Port Said the Waughs had run out of money. He-Evelyn's old university friend Alastair Graham, who was living in Athens, was appealed to, and leant them some money to tide them over. When She-Evelyn was better the Waughs completed their cruise on another ship, and returned to London in April. The ensuing travel book, *Labels*, was published in 1930.

By the time the cruise had ended He-Evelyn was desperately in need of money and so immediately started work on a new novel, *Vile Bodies*, a satire on the life of the Bright Young Things of 1920s London. He also managed to get some work as a reviewer for *The Observer* and *The Evening Standard*, but he did not enjoy writing articles. The comic novel was much more his thing. Many of the characters and events in *Vile Bodies* are based in part on real people and real happenings, with Diana Guinness being to some extent the model for the society hostess Margot Metroland, and the two gossip columnists for the 'Daily Excess' being based partly on Patrick Balfour (later Lord Kinross) who was at that time the gossip columnist for the *Daily Sketch*, and Tom Driberg who was writing for the *Daily Express*. The Bright Young Things go to lots of parties including masked parties, savage parties, Wild West parties, parties in swimming baths and parties where one has to dress as somebody else. The Prime Minister's daughter is one of the Bright Young Things and he is forced to resign when the newspapers report on the goings on at Number 10. The gossip columnist invents fashion fads and imaginary people and eventually gets the sack after advocating the wearing of bottle green bowler hats.

Evelyn found that living in a small flat with She-Evelyn was not conducive to writing, and so started spending week-days at an old haunt, the Abingdon Arms in Beckley, only returning to London at weekends. She-Evelyn's friend Nancy Mitford moved into the London flat to keep her company, and they used to entertain a lot. Two friends who were frequent visitors to the flat were Anthony Powell and John Heygate, both of whom had been at Eton and Balliol College, Oxford. To cut a long story short, She-Evelyn fell in love with John Heygate and went to live with him. He-Evelyn was absolutely devastated and filed for divorce. Nancy Mitford distanced herself from her erstwhile friend and became instead a friend and correspondent of He-Evelyn.

Nancy and Evelyn Waugh had moved in the same circles ever since she came out as a débutante and they knew many of the same people including John Betjeman, Cyril Connolly, Robert Byron and Harold Acton. For several years after the breakup of Evelyn's marriage they often met at cocktail parties, fancy dress parties, the theatre, and country house parties. Evelyn encouraged Nancy to write and she provided light articles for *Vogue, Harper's Bazaar* and *The Lady*. After Nancy's marriage to Peter Rodd, however, Evelyn and Nancy saw very little of each other as Evelyn had known Peter at Oxford and very much disliked him. After his wife left him Evelyn was invited by his friends Bryan and Diana Guinness to stay at their seaside home in Sussex to finish *Vile Bodies* and he accepted, gratefully dedicating the book to them. He could not resist introducing a character called Ginger Littlejohn, who was based on John Heygate, into his novel. In the novel Nina, who is not in love with Ginger, marries him solely for his money. She-Evelyn would later appear in the guise of Celia in the novel *Brideshead Revisited*.

Possibly as a result of the traumatic end to his marriage Evelyn converted to Catholicism and on 29th September 1930 he was received into the Roman Catholic Church. His Catholicism would influence the rest of his literary career, with the theme of Catholic guilt never far below the surface in the plots of most of his subsequent novels. He also disapproved of the welfare state and the growth of popular culture, and believed that the Catholic Church might in some way stand up against both of these. Shortly after his conversion Evelyn went to Ethiopia (then known as Abyssinia) as a journalist to cover the coronation of Haile Selassie. He went on to travel through British East Africa and the Belgian Congo, a journey which resulted in the travel book *Remote People* and the comic novel *Black Mischief* concerning the efforts of the Emperor Seth to modernise his empire. The emperor is assisted in his efforts by Basil Seal, who is based in part on Nancy Mitford's husband, Peter Rodd. An old acquaintance from Evelyn's Oxford days, Basil Murray, also contributed to the character of Basil.

* * * * *

By October 1931 Evelyn was homeless and divorced. When he was taking riding lessons near Malvern he was invited to dine at nearby Madresfield Court, the home of the Lygon family. He had been friendly during his time at Oxford University with both Hugh Lygon and his elder brother, Lord Elmley. Their father had recently gone into exile abroad after a homosexual scandal, their mother was living with her brother the Duke of Westminster, and the only permanent residents of Madresfield apart from the servants were the two youngest daughters Lady Mary (known as Maimie) and Lady Dorothy (known as Coote). Hugh was an intermittent visitor when he was between ventures. Cheery company was just what Evelyn needed at this time, and he soon fell in love with both the house and the family. The sisters enjoyed his first visit and invited him for several lengthy stays over the next couple of years. Evelyn played childish pranks on them and they regarded him as an indulgent uncle. Coote said later that it was like having Puck living with them. Madresfield Court provided Evelyn with the peace and quiet he needed for his writing. While staying there he wrote both *Remote People* and *Black Mischief*, and he dedicated *Black Mischief* to the sisters. It was Madresfield Court and the family who lived there which would provide the basis for Evelyn's best-known novel, *Brideshead Revisited*. Maimie, who formed a close friendship with Evelyn, inspired the character of Julia in the novel, and Coote was the model for her younger sister Cordelia. The art nouveau chapel at Brideshead is based on the chapel at Madresfield, which had been redecorated by the sisters' mother, Lady Lettice, as a wedding present for her husband.

* * * * *

The winter of 1932-33 saw Evelyn off on his travels again, this time to South America. The resultant novel, *A Handful of Dust,* was inspired by his visits to British Guiana and Brazil. In the novel Tony Last, whose wife has been unfaithful to him, joins an expedition to the Brazilian jungle where he and the leader of the group, Dr Messinger, are abandoned by their native guides. Tony falls ill, and when Dr Messinger sets off in a canoe to get help he is carried over a waterfall and killed. Tony is delirious but is eventually rescued and nursed back to health by a British settler, Mr Todd, and condemned to read and re-read the Complete Works of Dickens to Mr Todd for the rest of his life.

In August 1935, after completing a biography of the Catholic martyr Edmund Campion, Evelyn went to Abyssinia to report on the Italo-Abyssinian War for the *Daily Mail*. William Deedes (who would later become editor of *The Daily Telegraph* and the Bill to whom *Private Eye*'s Dear Bill letters were written by a spoof Denis Thatcher during the

Thatcher years) was a fellow reporter. Evelyn's novel *Scoop* is based on their visit. In the novel the well-connected socialite Mrs Stitch (based on Lady Diana Cooper) is asked to find work as a foreign correspondent for a novelist whose name is Boot. She arranges for the eccentric newspaper proprietor Lord Copper of the *Daily Beast* (who seems to be a mixture of Lord Beaverbrook and Lord Northcliffe) to send Boot to cover the war in Ishmaelia, but unfortunately the wrong Boot is sent. William Boot, the newspaper's nature correspondent, is a retiring country gentleman who writes weekly articles on British wildlife using such phrases as 'feather-footed through the plashy fen passes the questing vole'. William is partially based on William Deedes, who as a young, inexperienced reporter arrived in Addis Ababa with 600 pounds of luggage. In the novel William accidentally manages to get a scoop for his newspaper, but the other Boot gets the credit and William returns to his quiet life in the country. A General Cruttwell makes a cameo appearance in the novel.

Evelyn also wrote a book, *Waugh in Abyssinia,* about his experiences in that country. The book gives an interesting account of how the Italians came to be in Abyssinia, and describes the Italian invasion with warmth and humour. Evelyn found little evidence that there was a war going on, and consequently there was not much to report on. He heard some supposedly first-hand accounts of the blowing up of a hospital, but then discovered that it hadn't actually happened. When he received a telegram from London asking for the name and life story of a nurse who was blown up, he was mindful of the fact that telegrams were charged by the word and replied with the two words 'Nurse unupblown'.

* * * * *

By 1936 Evelyn had become a successful writer, but he felt that his private life was unsatisfactory. Ever since his failed marriage he had been of no fixed abode, staying in the houses of various friends and relations between his trips abroad. What he wanted, or at least thought that he wanted, was family life and stability. Help was at hand in the form of Laura Herbert, the third and youngest daughter of the Conservative MP Aubrey Herbert, who had died in 1923. Laura was thirteen years younger than Evelyn and very shy, but he gradually became enamoured of her. Evelyn had first met the Catholic Herbert family as long ago as 1933 while on a cruise of the Greek islands, and in 1934 was invited to stay at the family home, Pixton Park in Somerset. After that he met up with Laura at irregular intervals, sometimes in London, and kept up a correspondence with her, but had to wait until 1936 for the annulment of his first marriage. He proposed to Laura by letter in the spring of that year, and they were married in April 1937. Mrs Herbert had at first been opposed to the marriage because Evelyn was middle class, and Evelyn himself warned Laura that his only income came from his writing so that if he became ill they would stave, but neither of these issues was sufficient to prevent matrimony. As a wedding present Laura's grandmother gave them Piers Court, a country house near Stinchcombe in Gloucestershire which Evelyn used to refer to as 'Stinkers'. He had long dreamed of becoming a country squire, and was in his element. Over the years he gradually filled the house with Victorian paintings and furniture, often bought from house clearance sales. Evelyn and Laura would go on to have seven children (one of whom died in infancy). Laura settled down to a quiet life managing a country house, and took to raising cattle as a hobby. But Evelyn did not find that family life and writing mixed well. He soon realised that he didn't actually like children very much, and as each child reached the age of seven it was packed off to boarding school and only allowed home in the school holidays. At the end of each holiday Evelyn would celebrate wildly, much to the distress of the children. As the children grew older he made use of them to play some of his beloved practical jokes on his friends, on one occasion persuading them to hide behind bushes in the garden and pop up shouting 'Cyril Connolly, I presume!' each time Cyril walked past. It was only when the children grew older that Evelyn began to pay them much attention.

During the second half of 1937 Evelyn wrote a weekly series of book reviews for a new magazine called *Night and Day* which had been founded in July 1937 as a literary rival to *Punch*. Graham Greene, a fellow Catholic author, was one of the editors, and another editor was the travel writer Peter Fleming. John Betjeman also had a weekly column, Graham Greene himself wrote film reviews, and the novelist Elizabeth Bowen was the magazine's drama critic. The short-lived magazine was forced to close in December 1937 when it lost its financial backing after a libel action involving a Greene review of a Shirley Temple film. Meanwhile Evelyn continued writing book reviews and other articles for the Catholic paper *The Tablet*, including a critical review of the structure of Cyril Connolly's autobiographical *Enemies of Promise*. After the war Evelyn resumed writing for *The Tablet*, and in 1946 reviewed Orwell's *Critical Essays*.

In 1938 Evelyn and Laura went to Mexico for three months, and afterwards he wrote *Robbery Under Law* which was based on his experiences there. The book deals with the nationalisation of the petroleum industry by the left-wing government, and the persecution of Mexican Catholics.

* * * * *

When World War Two broke out Evelyn sent his wife and children to live with Laura's mother in Somerset, and in December 1939 he joined the Royal Marines. He trained at Chatham naval base and in April 1940 he was promoted to captain and put in charge of a company of marines, but he was unpopular with his men who didn't like his haughtiness and he lost his temporary promotion. Instead he was made the battalion's intelligence officer. In the autumn of 1940 he saw service in West Africa, then was sent to a commando unit and involved in the evacuation of Crete in 1941. On the journey home in July 1941 he wrote the novel *Put Out More Flags*, which is about the early years of the war.

Put Out More Flags is a grim satire on war, without much in the way of plot. In the novel Basil Seal, who is one of the Bright Young Things, reappears. Basil is bored, so agrees to help his sister Barbara place evacuees with rural families. He manages to turn this process into a business – country house residents are happy to pay Basil not to bring unruly children to live with them. In the end Basil redeems himself by joining the commandos. Alastair Trumpington, who was a student in *Decline and Fall*, reappears as a serious person who volunteers for army life, but he goes on lots of manoeuvres instead of being engaged in real combat. The two writers Parsnip and Pimpernel go to the United States to avoid the war. *Put Out More Flags* is the last of Evelyn's satirical novels – his later works would be much more serious.

In May 1942 Evelyn was transferred to the Royal Horse Guards. He had to take leave to deal with the death of his father, then sustained a broken leg during parachute training. As a result of this he took six months unpaid leave to write a book. The resultant novel was *Brideshead Revisited*, the most well-known and best loved of all Evelyn's works. In Mid 1944 Randolph Churchill arranged a posting for Evelyn and himself with a military mission in Yugoslavia. Evelyn's main duty was to liaise between the British Army and the Communist partisans. As a devout Catholic Evelyn did not approve of the way Catholics were treated in Yugoslavia and he wrote a report about the matter, but the Foreign Office suppressed the report in order to maintain good relations with Tito.

It was while Evelyn was stationed in Yugoslavia that he began a correspondence with Nancy Mitford which would continue until his death more than 20 years later. In London during 1942-3 he had got into the habit of popping into Heywood Hill's bookshop where Nancy worked, and had resumed his old friendship with her. An added tie was that Randolph Churchill was her cousin. Nancy would supply Evelyn with reading material from the shop, and they began to exchange views on the books that the two of them had been reading. They discovered that she liked Nabokov's Lolita and he didn't, and he didn't think much of Kingsley Amis and Lucky Jim either. Later Evelyn was asked to review Cyril Connolly's *The Unquiet Grave* for *The Tablet*. He was very disparaging about the book, telling Nancy that he thought Cyril needed to spend more time in White's (the most exclusive of the London clubs) in order to civilise himself. Evelyn and Nancy shared the same very idiosyncratic sense of humour, a humour which is present throughout their correspondence. Nancy's letters also included gossip, often exaggerated, about mutual acquaintances such as Alan Lennox-Boyd. Alan had gone for a 'flu vaccination and afterwards he felt very unwell when he was in a committee meeting at the House of Commons. Suddenly he heard the man sitting opposite to him telling the committee chairman that he felt as though he was going mad because Alan seemed to have swollen to twice his normal size. According to Nancy, Alan had actually increased in size because the doctor had given him elephantiasis by mistake, and he was taken away to lie on four beds with his trunk hanging out of the window (Gerald Berners, on hearing the tale, asked to be told if Chips Channon turned into an animal too because it would be worthwhile going to see him).

As well as exchanging gossip Nancy and Evelyn also exchanged notes on how they were getting on with their respective books, and became literary mentors to each other.

Nancy would send Evelyn the manuscripts of her books for him to comment on, and in return for his advice she let him know what people thought about his books. Her feedback on *Brideshead Revisited* included the statements that Raymond Mortimer considered it a Great English Classic, Cyril Connolly didn't like the 'purple passages' such as the deathbed scene, Osbert Sitwell was jealous that Evelyn could write so well, and Maurice Bowra thought that Evelyn was showing off but was still impressed by the book. People in general, said Nancy, thought that there was too much Catholicism in the book.

As well as writing to Nancy about literature, Evelyn did not hesitate to tell her what he really thought about other things such as art and politics. After visiting an exhibition of Picasso's work he described the artist as a 'counter-hon', opining that the Cubists were anti-painters whose pictures were bought by lunatics. As far as politics were concerned, Evelyn spoke out against what he considered to be Nancy's communist views and she countered by saying that she was a socialist, not a communist. Evelyn and Nancy had a lot in common, including a shared sense of humour and a nostalgia for the upper class way of life which was coming to an end, but they found they got on better as correspondents than they did when they actually met in person. When Evelyn visited Nancy in Paris they often quarrelled as he was very bad-tempered and her wit could be unkind. On one occasion in 1949 they called on the Duff Coopers and Evelyn was so argumentative that Nancy felt completely humiliated. The following year he was so rude to all her friends that she asked him how he reconciled his bad behaviour with being a Christian (he said that his behaviour would be even worse if he wasn't one). Eventually she realised that he wasn't rude to duchesses, only to middle class intellectuals.

But to return to *Brideshead Revisited.* In the novel Evelyn clearly outlines his religious belief that man cannot live without God. The narrator, Charles Ryder, is in love with the whole Flyte family of Catholics and their beautiful home. At first his fascination is mainly with his Oxford friend Sebastian, the younger son of the family, but after Sebastian succumbs to the demon drink and moves abroad Charles turns his attentions to Sebastian's sister Julia. Julia marries a brash American divorcee and after a rather squalid marriage realises that she has made a terrible mistake. She has an affair with Charles and is on the point of marrying him (he has by then divorced his shallow society wife) when she realises that she cannot estrange herself from her Catholic faith by divorce and remarriage.

As usual in Evelyn's novels the settings and characters are drawn from real life. The Lygon family home, Madresfield Court in Worcestershire, is the basis for the Flyte family's house, Brideshead Castle, although some of the descriptions of the exterior match those of Castle Howard in Yorkshire, which Evelyn had visited in March 1937. Charles and Sebastian's stay in Venice is modelled on a visit to that city made by Evelyn and his friend Mary Lygon in 1932. The lives of the Lygon family members are not replicated exactly in the novel, however. For example the real Lord Beauchamp had been forced into exile abroad because of his homosexuality whereas in the book Lord Marchmain is living in Venice with his mistress. Beauchamp's deathbed scene is based on that of Hubert Duggan, a lapsed Catholic who received the last rites and repented of all the years he had spent with his mistress (Evelyn had been present at his death). Lord Elmley is undoubtedly the model for Lord Beauchamp's oldest son, although in real life it was Evelyn's friend Richard Plunket- Greene who collected matchboxes. The rest of the Flyte family, too, were based on members of the Lygon family, with Hugh providing the basis for Sebastian, the good-looking and good-natured younger son who doesn't need to earn a living. Sebastian's sisters Julia and Cordelia are partially modelled on Mary and Dorothy Lygon. Two of the other people in the novel are also taken from real life. Anthony Blanche, the gay man who declaims poetry through a megaphone, is a mixture of Evelyn's Oxford friends Harold Acton and Brian Howard. Harold had recited poetry from his balcony at the hearties going down to the river to row, but Anthony's camp clothes and biting wit are those of Brian Howard. Sebastian's German friend Kurt is based on Brian Howard's German boyfriend Toni Altmann.

* * * * *

The publication of *Brideshead Revisited* in 1945 made Evelyn rich and famous and assured his place in history as a great literary figure. In February 1947 he was invited to the United States to discuss the filming of the book, but he didn't like the fact that the Americans wanted to adapt it and that they saw it purely as a love story. The idea for a film was abandoned, but while Evelyn was in Hollywood he visited the Forest Lawn Cemetery which gave him the basis for his book on the American way of death, *The Loved One*, a satire on the shallowness of life in Los Angeles. The action takes place mainly in two funeral parlours, one for humans and one for pets. Most of the protagonists are fighting to maintain their place in society, and the employees of the human cemetery look down on the employees of the pet cemetery. The complicated plot ends with one of the characters, who has committed suicide, being secretly cremated at the pet cemetery in order to avoid a scandal. *The Loved One* took up the whole of the February 1948 edition of *Horizon*, the literary magazine edited by Cyril Connolly.

Evelyn's next published book was *Helena*, a novel about St. Helena who was the mother of the Roman Emperor Constantine. She was allegedly the discoverer of the True Cross. Constantius, Helena's husband, seems to be based on

Field-Marshal Montgomery, whom Evelyn disliked and considered to be an arrogant social climber. (In contrast Nancy Mitford, meeting Montgomery at a dinner party given by the Gladwyn Jebbs, found him charming, or, to use her word, 'divine', and regularly dined with him at the Jebbs' after Gladwyn became Ambassador to Paris).

The *Sword of Honour* trilogy, which is loosely based on Evelyn's experiences in the war, soon followed *Helena*. It consisted of *Men at Arms* (published in 1952), *Officers and Gentlemen* (published in 1955), and *Unconditional Surrender* (published in 1961). The novels follow the fortunes of Guy Crouchback, who is from a declining upper class English Catholic family.

By January 1954 Evelyn's health was not good and his doctors suggested a trip abroad. He took a boat to Ceylon, but on board he began hearing voices and thought that the other passengers were whispering about him, so he left the boat when it reached Egypt and went on to Colombo by air. He then thought that he was possessed by devils, but despite this he managed to make his way home. It turned out that Evelyn had been suffering from bromide poisoning, apparently provoked by his sleeping tablets. Once his medication was changed the voices soon went away. The result of this experience was the semi-autobiographical book *The Ordeal of Gilbert Pinfold*, in which Evelyn describes what happened to him. The book received mixed reviews. J B Priestley, who reviewed it for *The New Statesman*, decried the fact that Evelyn was trying to combine the roles of author and landed Catholic gentleman.

Evelyn had been dissatisfied with life at his home Piers Court for some time, partly because uninvited visitors were disturbing the tranquillity of his life there, but also due to the fact that suburbia was encroaching on the area. In 1955 he and Laura went house hunting in Devon and Cornwall and in 1956 they found a suitable 18th-century house, Combe Florey, which was actually in Somerset. They moved in in October. In defiance of J B Priestley and partly in order to prove his own staunch Catholicism, Evelyn soon afterwards started work on a biography of Ronald Knox, the Catholic writer and theologian whom he had known personally and who had recently died. The biography is somewhat odd in that Evelyn describes Knox's Eton and Oxford days in detail but glosses over his personal life and his most important achievement, ie his translation of the Bible into modern English. Evelyn's friend Christopher Sykes thought that this was because Evelyn considered the translation to be purely literal and lacking in poetry (Evelyn himself had described the translation in a 1948 issue of *Horizon* as 'grimly functional'). Perhaps he was ashamed that the man he considered a hero had produced such mundane prose. The book did not do very well, with Evelyn himself describing it as selling 'like warm cakes'.

Both Ronald Knox and Evelyn liked to keep their personality and their private life away from the public gaze. When Evelyn was interviewed on BBC television in 1960 the questioner tried to get him to discuss his life as a country gentleman. Evelyn admitted that he had no interest in agriculture or local government, and said that what he liked about the countryside was that he could be silent there. After Evelyn had maintained that he had no interest in being famous an interviewer asked why, therefore, he had agreed to appear on television. Evelyn replied with one word - 'Poverty' (Although his books sold well and he was well remunerated for his newspaper and magazine articles, Evelyn was always short of money due to his extravagant lifestyle, and in 1950 he had set up a trust fund for his children which he called the 'Save the Children Fund'). 1960 saw the publication of Evelyn's final travel book, *A Tourist in Africa*, which was based on a trip he made between January and March 1959. Evelyn's old Oxford friend, Cyril Connolly, thought it the least well-written of all his books.

By 1962 Evelyn was in poor health. He was fat and rather deaf, and had been having a lot of trouble with his false teeth. He also drank a lot and was becoming increasingly grumpy. He was becoming his own public persona. His bad temper and rudeness offended lots of people and made him many enemies, although according to friends his antagonism towards strangers was really just him looking for someone to stand up to him so that he could enjoy a good argument. Nancy Mitford maintained that everything about Evelyn was just a joke, and that no-one seemed to take that into account. Her sister Deborah, who knew Evelyn well, said that he was only grumpy when he drank, but that unfortunately he drank most of the time. Evelyn's brother Alec said that Evelyn gave the impression of being heartless and cruel but that underneath he was warm and gentle, a statement which seems to be borne out by the fact that he had lots of friends and was generous to both individual people and good causes. What does seem to be true, however, is that he disliked the proletarian masses and believed that class divisions and inequalities of wealth were natural phenomena, though he was apolitical and never voted in elections. He thought that society needed to be organised hierarchically in order to function. His novel *Love Among the Ruins: a Romance of the Near Future* of 1953 portrays a society where everyone is equal and dependent on the welfare state. Because people are so unhappy the euthanasia service (which is not restricted to the terminally ill) becomes the most-used section of the welfare state. In 1960 Evelyn declined the CBE, thinking that he should have been given a knighthood.

Despite all his problems, in 1962 Evelyn managed to rouse himself sufficiently to write one last story, *Basil Seal Rides Again*. It is subtitled 'The Rake's Progress'. Basil is now 60 and partially based on Evelyn himself – they are both fat, deaf and short of breath. Basil has become a respected member of society and has joined a London club. He is happily married to Angela (her first husband was killed in the war) and they have plenty of money. The poets Parsnip and Pimpernel have both become professors at American universities. In the same year Evelyn started work on his autobiography and the first volume, *A Little Learning,* was published in 1964 (luckily for his friends he did not use their real names and so they were not too embarrassed by tales of their indiscretions). That year Evelyn also wrote to *The Spectator* to complain about the decision of the Second Vatican Council to celebrate mass in the vernacular, and he also moaned about it in letters to his old friend Nancy Mitford. Due to his declining health Evelyn was unable to do any further work on either his autobiography or the other books which he had been contracted to write, and he died at his home on 10th April 1966.

CHAPTER SIX – ROBERT BYRON

Robert Byron (1905-41) was a traveller writer, art historian and campaigner for the preservation of old buildings both at home and abroad. He is best remembered today for his book *The Road to Oxiana*.

* * * * *

Robert Henry Byron was born on 26th February 1905 in Wembley. He had two younger sisters, Anne and Lucy. His father, Eric, was working as a civil engineer at that time. The family were distantly related to Lord Byron. Robert's mother, Margaret, had a talent for painting and had studied at South Kensington School of Art, and it was from her that Robert inherited his artistic ability and his great intelligence. Robert's paternal grandfather owned a large estate, Coulsdon Court in Surrey, and although Eric was the youngest of three sons it was expected that he would inherit the estate as his older brothers had emigrated to Canada and were not interested in returning to England. However, in 1920 Eric's sister Lucy persuaded their father, Edmund, to alter his will. The new will stipulated that when Edmund died the whole estate should be sold and the proceeds divided between his various heirs. The heirs included Lucy, her sister Eva, her brother Eric, and a Canadian grandchild. Edmund died in 1921 and the estate was indeed sold. Most of the farm land was auctioned off in lots, and the house and grounds eventually became a hotel and golf course.

Eric already had an income from his investments and after World War One he no longer needed to earn his living as an engineer. In 1919 the family began renting a house at Knowle on the eastern edge of Savernake Forest in Wiltshire. Eric had enjoyed exploring the forest as a schoolboy while at Marlborough College. The family later took a long lease on Savernake Lodge, a substantial old hunting lodge in the forest which had been partially destroyed by fire in 1861 and was known locally as 'The Ruins'. The house had no electricity and was very cold, but the Byrons loved its location deep in the forest and down a track half a mile from the nearest road. Eric threw himself into rural life with enthusiasm and constructed a garden and a tennis court for the house. He had become a country gentleman after all.

From an early age Robert developed an interest in the countryside. He and his mother often stayed with his grandfather at Coulsdon, where she took him for long walks and taught him the names of the wild flowers. His love of nature and his closeness to his mother would stay with him all his life. On National Poetry Day in October 2006 his (only) poem *All These I Learnt,* which was written for his mother, was chosen by the BBC to be broadcast on Radio 4. The poem lovingly details the flowers he saw, giving them their old country names such as dog's mercury and lady's bedstraw, and telling how Robert intended to pass on his enthusiasm to the son he hoped to have. Although Robert does not seem to have been emotionally attached to his father he enjoyed spending time with him as well as with his mother, and after Robert learnt to ride he and his father would go out hunting and shooting together.

When Robert was three his mother taught him to read using the Peter Rabbit books. She had kept up her interest in painting after her marriage, and encouraged her son to draw and paint from an early age. The pair often visited the National Gallery together, and Margaret sometimes copied the old masters in oils. Perhaps it was his early visits to the gallery with his mother which gave Robert his aversion to the gloomy paintings of Rembrandt and his life-long love of colour. His mother may also have been the cause of his indifference to Shakespeare, as she forced him to learn long passages of the bard's work by heart. Robert's love of colour was fuelled by his admiration for his grandparents' elegant furniture and porcelain.

At the age of eleven Robert was sent away to boarding school in Worcestershire, where he spent his free time going for long walks in the countryside and drawing the plants and animals he saw there. He also had formal art lessons at school. He was extremely bright and easily passed the scholarship examination for Eton, but was unable to take up a scholarship due to lack of places. His mother eventually managed to persuade his grandfather to pay the full fees, and he started at Eton in January 1919. He enjoyed studying history and became a proficient essay-writer, winning a prize for one of his essays. He continued to draw in his free time and also took extra drawing lessons with Sidney Evans, the chief drawing master, at 'The Studio'. It was during his time at Eton that Robert began to be interested in architecture, spending many of his free afternoons sketching the school buildings and nearby Windsor Castle. While drawing at The Studio Robert met several boys who were to become life-long friends, including Harold Acton and Brian Howard who invited him to join their newly-formed Eton Society of Arts. The aim of the Society was to foster an interest in listening to music, looking at pictures, and reading poetry. Harold and Brian were already writing their own verse, and the other members of the Society were keen artists. Most of the members were averse to team sports and were keen to belong to an organisation where sport was not considered the be-all and end-all of life . The Society had weekly meetings at which members took it in turn to present papers on different aspects of art. Robert liked realism in art and spoke in defence of Ruskin and Victorianism, arguing against Harold and Brian who preferred the Post-Impressionists. But Robert considered that his greatest triumph was securing a visit to the Society from Sir William Rothenstein, who was then the principal of the Royal College of Art.

Although Robert was not interested in team sports he was wiry and quite athletic. He took up cross country running and won at least one cup for it. He was allowed to take rowing instead of cricket, and to participate in beagling. It was while beagling that he made a new friend, Henry Yorke, who would later go on to write novels under the pseudonym Henry Green. Robert was invited to stay with the Yorke family at their London house and there he made another friend, Henry's mother. Maud Yorke was one of the Wyndhams and had been brought up at Petworth. She and Robert shared a love of the decorative arts and she enjoyed showing him round her Robert Adam house with its Angelica Kauffmann ceilings. Robert also went to stay with the Yorkes at their country home, Forthampton Court near Tewkesbury. Robert's other friends were mainly in Robeson's House, where he lived, and included Rudolph Messel and Rudolph's cousin the future theatre designer Oliver Messel, and John Spencer with whom Robert messed, ie had tea. John, who was a great dandy and rule-breaker, encouraged Robert to dress up with him and indulge in various pranks. John sent off to Scotland for some brightly-patterned tweed and Robert had some plus fours made from it. The pair also enjoyed choosing accessories such as silk ties, silk socks, suede gloves and brightly coloured handkerchiefs. Robert was indulging his new-found love of textiles to the full, and embarrassing his mother on holidays such as the Fourth of June. John was eventually expelled from Eton for getting drunk at an OTC camp. Robert began to enjoy breaking the rules too, on one occasion putting up an umbrella when it rained while he was on OTC parade. With his friend Cecil Clonmore he indulged in the forbidden vices of smoking and drinking, and the duo would wander round Slough openly smoking and then stroll into one of the local pubs for a glass of beer. Despite all his extra-curricular activities Robert easily passed the Oxford University Entrance Examination, and in January 1923 he went up to Merton College to read Modern History.

* * * * *

Cecil Clonmore and Rudolph Messel were already up at Merton and they introduced Robert to their set, which included the old Etonians David Talbot Rice, John Heygate, Gavin Henderson and Alfred Duggan. Robert was soon going to parties and dance halls with them, and attending elaborate luncheon parties in their rooms. He wrote home to his mother telling her that it was very difficult to find time to do any work. Robert's friend from the Eton Society of Arts, Harold Acton, was also up at Oxford. Arriving at Christ Church in October 1922, Harold chose rooms in Meadow Buildings overlooking Christ Church Meadow because he wanted a view. He immediately set about decorating his rooms with Victorian objets d'art in keeping with the Gothic revival style of the building. Robert soon embraced Harold's mania for collecting Victorian things and enjoyed searching in junk shops for Berlin woolwork pictures and nineteenth-century glass domes and paperweights with which to embellish his rooms. His passion for collecting things had begun in a conventional way at prep school with the accumulation of fossils and coins. At Eton he had graduated to collecting decorative items such as candlesticks and paintings, and had enjoyed rummaging around in what would nowadays be called 'vintage' shops in Eton, Slough and Windsor. He was developing an eye for interior design. Harold, inspired by a visit to the 1840 Exhibition in Venice, thought it would be a good idea to show off their collection of Victoriana at a similar exhibition at their university, and he and Robert eagerly set about trying to arrange this. They persuaded some of their acquaintances to lend items such as pictures and statues for the exhibition, and Robert invited Lytton Strachey to write a foreword for the programme, though he graciously declined to do so. Advertisements for the forthcoming exhibition were placed in the student magazine *The Cherwell*, which was edited by Robert's friend John Sutro, but in the end the authorities banned the exhibition on the grounds that it was unnecessary.

Harold, like Robert, enjoyed dressing up and ignoring conventions. Robert and Harold, together with their new friend Evelyn Waugh, would order items from their tailors which were designed to shock both by their style and their colour. Wearing jackets with wide lapels and those wide-legged trousers which became known as Oxford bags, they paraded round Oxford. Robert also frequented fancy dress parties at The Hypocrites Club, where he sometimes dressed as Queen Victoria whom he had been told that he resembled. He also sang Victorian music hall songs and accompanied himself on the piano. Later he joined John Sutro's Railway Club and enjoyed going on excursions by train and eating extensive dinners in the dining car. He never lost his childish sense of humour, and on one occasion when the Club visited the Station Hotel at Paddington he swapped round all the pairs of shoes which people had left outside their rooms to be polished. You might think that by the time he was in his final year at Oxford Robert would knuckle down and do some work towards his degree, especially as he was away from the influence of his student peers and sharing rooms in Beaumont Street with John Sutro. However, his friend David Plunket Greene had just returned from America with jazz records, poloneck sweaters and recipes for cocktails, so Robert's life continued much as before. Roy Harrod, then a young don at Oxford, remembers long lunches in John Sutro's rooms where Robert and his friends would spend hours discussing how to put the world to rights.

At Easter 1923 Robert was invited to go to Italy with Lord Beauchamp and his two sons, Lord Elmley and Hugh Lygon. Hugh was an old Eton friend of Robert's, and had been a member of the

Eton Society of Arts. He was currently studying in Germany. The party visited Venice, Florence and Rome, but the highlight of the trip for Robert was a visit to the Church of Sant'Apollinaire Nuovo in Ravenna. It was his experience of seeing the wonderful mosaics there that first kindled his enthusiasm for Byzantine art, though he had already read some books about the Byzantine influence on Western art. A trip round Europe by train with Cecil Clonmore in the summer of 1924 did nothing to enhance Robert's view of abroad, but his enthusiasm revived when in August 1925 he and his friends Gavin Henderson and Alfred Duggan undertook an adventure which involved driving from London to Athens in Gavin's Sunbeam car. Their journey took them through Germany and Italy via Hamburg, Berlin, Munich, Rome and Brindisi. The trip was not without its problems, which included having to hang around in Bologna for a week waiting for a new carburettor, and finding on arrival in Patras that there was no actual road from there to Athens (Diana the Sunbeam had to be transported to Corinth by train). In his account of their travels in his first book, *Europe in the Looking Glass*, Robert tells us about adventures on dusty roads where punctures frequently occurred, and about the visit to Verona where they saw a performance of Rossini's *Moses* at the open air amphitheatre. Robert wrote a review of the opera which was published in *The Times*. The book also contains some lovely little drawings by Robert himself, including one of a portly gentleman (presumably Robert) helping to hoist Diana off a lighter.

In Athens the trio met up with a friend of Gavin's, Leonard Bower, with whom Robert enjoyed going round antique shops. Another of Gavin's friends, John Stuart Hay, was in Athens sorting out affairs to do with a bank partially owned by Gavin's grandfather. Contrary to his expectations (his mind had been blunted by old prints of ruins and broken pillars) Robert was thrilled by the Parthenon, though he was not interested in any of the other antiquities. He preferred visiting the Byzantine churches in the area. Robert was fascinated by the current political situation in Greece, and Leonard Bower took him to meet Dr Skevos Zervos, the exiled leader of the Association of the Dodecanese. After this meeting Robert wrote an article for the *New Statesman* about the injustices of Italian rule in the Dodecanese.

During Trinity Term 1925 Robert had actually got round to doing some revision for his History exams and he emerged from finals with a third class degree which he never bothered to collect. In order to qualify for a degree it was necessary to spend nine terms at Oxford, and Robert spent his final term in Autumn 1925 as editor of *The Cherwell*, for which he had already written articles in the past. He knew that he would have to start earning his living as soon as he left Oxford, and he also knew that he wanted to travel. It was his ambition to familiarise himself with the major civilisations of the world by the time he was thirty, and he felt that working as a journalist might provide him with the opportunity to do this. During his time at Oxford he had already written articles for various newspapers and magazines. *The Tatler* had printed an article by him about the Victorian revival in Oxford, for *The Daily Express* he had written in defence of the wearing of Oxford bags and poloneck sweaters, and *The Times* had published two items that he wrote about the situation in The Dodecanese. He had also written for *The New Statesman, The Daily Mail,* and the *Athenaeum.*

The Cherwell appeared sporadically, seemingly when its backer, John Sutro, had managed to pay the printer's bill for the previous edition. Robert had already contributed items to the magazine in the past, including an article on one of his Victorian domes and an item about the Oxford Union Debating Society. Even in those early days he was not afraid of controversy, and his statement that the Cambridge debating society was much better than the Oxford one had elicited a lot of complaints. He now took advantage of his position as editor of the magazine to write a series of articles about the plight of the Greeks in the Dodecanese who were living under Italian rule. He also did a favour to his old friend Henry Yorke, who was now up at Magdalen, by writing a review in praise of Henry's first novel, *Blindness*. The novel, written under the pseudonym Henry Green and penned mainly while Henry was still at Eton, concerns the childhood and youth of a boy called John Haye. Haye is based on Henry himself, and Eton and the Eton Society of Arts are thinly disguised in the novel. The character of Ben Gore, usually referred to in the book as BG, is based on Robert. After Haye is blinded in an accident he is convinced that BG is the only person who can understand how is feeling. Robert, acknowledging his thanks to Henry for portraying him favourably, signed the review BG. When Robert's first book, *Europe in the Looking Glass*, was published in 1926 Henry gave it a marvellous review and described it as 'brilliant'.

* * * * *

In January 1926, having left Oxford, Robert moved to London and managed to get a job as a trainee reporter on *The Daily Mail*. He was supposed to produce minor items of news which could be used to fill up any spare column inches, but instead of restricting himself to the facts he often ended up writing an essay. As a consequence his articles often had to be rewritten by someone else. He was also still writing for *The Cherwell*, whose readers appreciated news from London about fashion, new dance crazes and the latest cocktail recipes. After two months *The Daily Mail* decided to dispense with Robert's services, and he took advantage of the free time that this afforded to finish writing up *Europe in the Looking Glass*.

In May 1926 Robert returned to mainland Greece and visited the ruined Byzantine town of Mistra in the Peloponnese. He was horrified to find that the churches were all roofless and that rain and wind were ruining all their beautiful frescoes which were hundreds of years old. The following year he returned to Mistra to photograph them. Robert seems to have been the first person who was interested in preserving the frescoes, and after he had publicised their plight in his book *The Birth of Western Painting* the cause was taken up by one of the Athenian newspapers. This led to a wealthy Greek benefactor donating funds for the restoration of the churches.

Robert's burgeoning interest in Byzantine frescoes made him long to visit Mount Athos, and this he managed to do in both August 1926 and August 1927. On the first trip he was accompanied by Bryan Guinness (an old Eton and Oxford friend) and John Stuart Hay (who spoke Greek), and on his second visit his travelling companions were three friends from his Oxford days Mark Ogilvie-Grant, David Talbot Rice, and Gerald Reitlinger. An account of the two visits to Mount Athos is combined in Robert's book *The Station*, where he details the adventures and hardships of the trip as well as giving us detailed information on the architecture and frescoes of the monasteries. His personality shines through in his amusing accounts of his mishaps and his dealings with the monks, but there is also a serious side to the book when he considers the architecture and history of the Athos peninsula.

Another book which resulted from the trips to Mount Athos

was *The Birth of Western Painting*, which has text by Robert and photographs by David Talbot Rice. In this idiosyncratic book Robert praises Byzantine art and skates over everything painted in the West between the sixteenth and nineteenth centuries. He went on to write a third book about Byzantine art and history, which he called *The Byzantine Achievement*. The research for this book consisted of Robert reading every book on The Byzantine Empire which The London Library and the library at the British Legation in Athens possessed. It is a scholarly work which deals with the history, trade and culture of Byzantium, and although Robert was only an amateur historian the book received favourable reviews.

In writing his books on Byzantine art and history Robert wanted to prove his theory that Byzantine art, via the paintings of El Greco, is the origin of Western art. After inspecting the mosaics and frescoes of Istanbul and Meteora, and travelling to Crete and Toledo to see the works of El Greco and his contemporaries, Robert was convinced that the elongated figures in El Greco's portraits derive from stylised pictures of earlier Byzantine saints. When he visited St Sophia, Istanbul in 1923 the Christian mosaics were still plastered over and the church was being used as a mosque, but by the time he returned in 1931 the mosaics were being uncovered thanks to the pressure he had exerted on his wealthy friends Emerald Cunard and Benjamin Guinness to provide funding. Robert was also instrumental in the restoration of the mosaics and frescoes at St Saviour in Chora, Istanbul, the funding for which was provided by his friend Mrs Otto Kahn, a wealthy American patron of the arts.

* * * * *

During the second half of the nineteen twenties Robert lived mainly in London between his foreign trips, though he also spent time with his parents in Wiltshire. Several of his close friends were also living in London and trying to make a living from writing or publishing. These included people such as John Betjeman, Anthony Powell, Cyril Connolly, Patrick Balfour (Lord Kinross), Harold Acton, Alan Pryce-Jones, Peter Quennell and Evelyn Waugh. Robert and his friends were some of the Bright Young Things who were notorious for their fancy dress parties and their pranks. In 1928 Robert was living just round the corner from Evelyn Waugh, of whom he saw a great deal at that time. Evelyn (known as He-Evelyn) was renting a flat in order to be near his fiancée Evelyn Gardner (She-Evelyn) who was sharing a flat with Pansy Pakenham. Both Evelyns were spending a lot of time at Robert's place, which Robert told his mother was because their own flats were so squalid (Robert himself was very particular). The Evelyns were facing opposition to their marriage from Lady Burghclere, who did not want a son in law who was neither rich nor aristocratic, so in May 1928 they married without telling her. She only found out about the wedding when He-Evelyn wrote to tell her about it afterwards. It was a very quiet affair and as they married by special license there were no banns. Harold Acton was best man, Robert gave the bride away, and Pansy Pakenham and Alec Waugh were the witnesses. When Robert went to collect She-Evelyn to take her to the church he was worried that she might not want to go; he thought that she was only marrying in order to escape having to go back and live with her mother. He may have been right, as after only fourteen months of marriage She-Evelyn ran off with John Heygate.

After 1930 Robert and He-Evelyn didn't see much of each other as they were both travelling abroad, and their friendship petered out. Relations between them seem to have cooled after Evelyn became a catholic (Robert, who was very idiosyncratic, had been very anti-catholic ever since he had read about the 1204 sack of Constantinople). Harold Acton also suffered a cooling off in his friendship with Evelyn and thought that Evelyn might be distancing himself from those who knew about his first marriage in order to try and forget about it and hush it up. In later life Evelyn strongly disapproved of Robert's outspoken views, and their friendship never recovered its intimacy.

Someone else who socialised with Robert and the Bright Young Things was Nancy Mitford. Nancy had met Robert a few times at parties and been attracted to him, and in the autumn of 1928 she brazenly wrote to invite him to spend a few days at Swinbrook with his friend Bryan Guinness, who was dating her sister Diana. The visit was a great success. Robert and Nancy got on extremely well as they both loved riding and shared the same sense of humour. They liked to indulge in witty repartee and were very good at it. Nancy enjoyed

Robert's visit hugely and wrote excitedly to her brother Tom about it afterwards. An added bonus for Nancy was that her father approved of Robert – Lord Redesdale was averse to most of the young men that Nancy brought to his house, but unlike the others Robert liked to get up early and go out hunting or shooting. During that first visit to Swinbrook Robert suggested going riding with Nancy and her brother Tom in Spain the following Easter, but in the event he went off to India instead and the Spanish trip never materialised. Nancy and Robert remained close friends, however, and saw a lot of each other whenever Robert was in Wiltshire. They kept up a correspondence until the end of Robert's life, and they sometimes met at country house parties or in London.

Albert Memorial Gates, the main character in Nancy's first novel *Highland Fling*, is based mainly on Robert (Nancy's pet name for Robert was Bertie). Albert is good at witty repartee and enjoys playing practical jokes on people (he dresses up as the castle ghost). He collects Victoriana, and is delighted to find a cache of Victorian items in the attic of the old Scottish castle where he is staying. He brings the glass domes, wax flowers, lacquer boxes (Robert learnt lacquering at Eton) and watercolour pictures downstairs to photograph, and when a fire breaks out in the castle he rushes to save the Victorian items above everything else. Robert's dislike of strait-laced conventionality is illustrated by the game of Lists played by the house guests where Albert suggests they make a list of embarrassing diseases, and the final reference to Robert's interests comes when Albert is reading a book on the Angevin kings which Jane (aka Nancy) finds so boring that she throws it out of the train window on the journey home.

Nancy's second novel, *Christmas Pudding,* was actually dedicated to Robert. The protagonists are guests at a Christmas house party in the Cotswolds. The main character Paul Fotheringay, who is poor but charming, has many of Robert's characteristics and has written a book about the Byzantine empire. Again there are references to Victoriana in Nancy's descriptions of the house, which has Victorian domes in the hall, beaded firescreens and Berlin woolwork pictures (Nancy found it very amusing that whereas most homes of the gentry had pictures of their owners' ancestors on the walls, Savernake Lodge had woolwork pictures).

Nancy admitted in later life that she had been in love with Robert and would have liked to marry him. Robert's male friends, who knew that he was essentially gay, were amazed at the way he and Nancy inter-reacted. They had never seen him like that with a woman before and thought that perhaps he would get married after all. Some of them even thought that the pair might be engaged, but when Robert began to spend long periods abroad his friendship with Nancy was maintained mainly through correspondence. He didn't approve of Nancy's boyfriend Hamish Erskine because he thought he didn't have any morals, and he was pleased when Nancy married Peter Rodd although he found him a bore.

After her marriage Nancy continued to write to Robert. Her husband Peter wasn't interested in her literary career, whereas Robert was enthusiastic about her progress. When she was editing the letters of her Stanley ancestors she kept him up to date on how she was getting on. When she found that she was pregnant in the summer of 1938 Robert was the first person she told, which certainly indicates that they had a close relationship. In June 1939 when Nancy's bulldog Millie had puppies she gave one of them to Robert to keep him company, choosing Agnes as being the most appropriate because she was very anti-appeasement like Robert. During the summer of 1940, when Robert was working at the BBC, Nancy took him in as a paying guest as her house was very conveniently situated near to his place of work. However, she had to ask him to leave after a few weeks as, in his usual outspoken way, he was very rude to her bridge-playing friends. Instead Robert went to lodge with his friend Patrick Balfour (Lord Kinross) who lived nearby. Nancy's final sight of Robert was when he put her on the number 6 bus outside C & A in Oxford Street, just before he went off to Liverpool in February 1941 to take a boat to Alexandria. After Robert's death Nancy always maintained that of all her friends who had died he was the one she missed the most because she had shared jokes with him.

Nancy was not the only woman who wanted to marry Robert. During the summer of 1932 he was contacted by Penelope Chetwode whom he had previously met in Delhi when her father was Commander-in-Chief of the British Army. When they were both back in England she had stayed at Savernake Lodge and gone out riding with Robert a couple of times. When Penelope showed him an article about Indian temple architecture which she had written he suggested that she take it to John Betjeman at the *Architectural Review*. In a letter she wrote to Robert, Penelope virtually propositioned him by mentioning that Osbert Sitwell had told her mother that he would be delighted if she married Robert. No doubt Robert was delighted when Penelope married John Betjeman. Penelope's mother was not delighted, however, apparently remarking that you invited that sort of person to dinner but you didn't marry them (she had approved of Robert because he was gentry).

* * * * *

In 1929 *The Daily Express* had paid for Robert to fly to Karachi (then in pre-partition India) in return for him writing some articles about his trip. He also wrote about the journey in his book *First Russia, Then Tibet*. In India Robert met up with Gavin Henderson and the two of them travelled round southern India and Ceylon. In October they were joined by Michael Rosse to travel to Tibet, a journey which started from Government House in Darjeeling where the chaos caused by a fire in the night and the setting off of a fire extinguisher by Gavin gave Robert ample material for an amusing letter home to his mother. In Tibet the friends followed the established trade route to the town of Gyantse and stayed in government bungalows, but Robert suffered from dreadful headaches due to the altitude, and they sometimes had to dismount from their ponies and wade through waist-high snow. The journey was anything but easy. Robert enjoyed the trip despite the hardships, and was interested to see how life was lived away from Western culture in a country where the wheel was unknown. He loved the colours and textures of the people's clothes, and when the group finally arrived in the town of Gyantse he discovered that he loved Tibetan architecture too and spent some time sketching and photographing the monasteries and houses.

When Robert returned to Delhi for Christmas 1929 the *Architectural Review* commissioned him to write a series of articles on Lutyens' New Delhi. He also took a lot of photographs to illustrate the articles. Robert loved the architecture of New Delhi, which he found to be an interesting mixture of Eastern and Western styles. While on an assignment working for the Burmah Shell oil company in Calcutta he took the opportunity to make two tours of northern India. His travels round India resulted in his book *An Essay on India*, in which he talks about the problems facing the country and tries to decide whether British rule has been a success. He criticises the British sense of racial superiority, but also dislikes the Indian attempt to break away from Eastern spirituality in favour of Western materialism.

In the first half of his book *First Russia, Then Tibet* Robert tells us about his visits to Russia and the Ukraine. He first visited Moscow in 1932, when he had been sent there by the *Architectural Review* to carry out a survey of buildings. While he was in Russia he also wanted to make a study of Russian art to prove his hypothesis that the painters of Russian icons and frescoes had been inspired by paintings from Mount Athos, Constantinople and Mistra. In Moscow the only modern building which caught his attention was Lenin's tomb in Red Square; he much preferred the Kremlin and its cathedrals, finding that seeing them in the falling snow was like being in a fantasy land. Seeing Rublev's icons in the Tretyakov Gallery more or less confirmed to Robert his theory about the origins of Russian religious art. In St Petersburg he was obliged to spend two days being shown round the Hermitage, and after day one he wrote home to his mother that there were only forty more Rembrandts to go. A visit to Novgorod cheered him up however, and he admired the onion domes of the eleventh-century cathedral. On a visit to small churches out in the countryside at Spas-Nereditsy and Volotovo he was fortunate to find scaffolding inside which enabled him to get a good look at all the frescoes. He noticed that the curly hair and white beards of David and Job were similar to some of those in frescoes which he had seen on Mount Athos, and he was thrilled that this seemed to confirm his ideas about the origins of Russian art. It was lucky for posterity that Robert photographed some of the frescoes as both churches sustained significant damage during World War Two.

* * * * *

From September 1933 until June 1934 Robert travelled in Persia and

Afghanistan with his friend Christopher Sykes. He kept a detailed journal during this trip and later used it as the basis for his most famous book, *The Road to Oxiana*. The book is both a travelogue and a detailed record of Islamic architecture. During his travels Robert took many photographs of mosques, tomb towers and archaeological sites. Many of these buildings have since deteriorated or been destroyed by the actions of weather or war. The photographs are thus a valuable historic record, and have been preserved at the Courtauld Institute. Robert also put his artistic ability to good use, making detailed sketches and coloured drawings of the buildings he saw (his photographs, of course, were black and white). The book also documents a vanished way of life as Robert records the customs of the people he meets and their colourful clothes. For his mother's benefit he describes the countryside through which he travels including the scenery, the wild flowers and the butterflies.

The mosques in Persia had only been opened to non-Moslems in 1931, and so Robert and Christopher visited places which few westerners had seen. Their travels in Persia took them to Teheran, Meshed, Nishapur, Zinjan, Tabriz and Isfahan among other places. In Afghanistan the places they visited included Kabul, Bamian, Kunduz, Mazar-i-Sharif and Ghazni. One of Robert's most daring escapades was to go to the Imam Reza shrine in Meshed disguised as a Persian – if he had been found out he might have been put to death as a non-believer. He also visited the Sheikh Lutfullah Mosque in Isfahan, one of the most splendid examples of Safavid architecture, and described the wonderful interior of the dome in great detail.

* * * * *

In September 1935 Robert went to St Petersburg as a *Times* correspondent. He had been asked to cover both the Third International Congress of Persian Art and Archaeology and a large exhibition of Persian art at the Hermitage museum. After visiting these he managed to get a two-month extension to his visa which enabled him to cross Siberia by train. En route he stopped off at Ekaterinburg and saw the house where the Russian royal family had been murdered, and he also visited Irkutsk which was still a quaint old town with wooden buildings. In Khabarovsk he spent more than a week trying to get a visa to China but in the end he gave up and went to Vladivostok instead, from where he was able to get to Peking via Korea and Manchuria.

On arriving in Peking in November Robert went to stay with Desmond Parsons, with whom he had been in love for ten years. Desmond had been living in Peking since April 1934 and had been learning Chinese. In May 1935 he went on an expedition to the remote Tun-Huang caves in Kansu province to photograph the Buddhist murals, and his photographs were of such good quality that they were accepted by the Courtauld Institute. At the caves Desmond was arrested and accused of stealing ancient Buddhist carvings (which of course he hadn't). He was imprisoned for two weeks and suffered an attack of dysentery, but after complaints by diplomats and the British press he was released. He was the younger brother of Robert's friend Michael Rosse, and was renting a house in Peking which Harold Acton had found for him just two minutes' walk away from his own house. Visiting Desmond at that time were Michael, his wife Anne, and Desmond and Michael's mother Lady De Vesci. Harold arranged sightseeing trips and visits to the theatre for the party, but Desmond who had been feeling unwell for several weeks was diagnosed with Hodgkins disease and the family decided to take him back to Europe for treatment. Robert, who had been so looking forward to spending some time alone with Desmond after his family had left, was devastated to be left alone in Desmond's large house.

Robert had to spend Christmas Day on his own, apart from the four servants, and subsequently developed a high fever followed by neuralgia. He was taken to the German hospital and gradually recovered sufficiently to finish writing his articles about Russia for *The Times*. He then sent home for his diaries and set about finishing the writing of *The Road to Oxiana*. Robert's old friend Gerald Reitlinger came out to Peking in February and also rented a house, but as Gerald and Harold couldn't stand each other Robert had to divide the hour he allowed himself for socialising each day and spend thirty minutes with each of them. He didn't keep a diary during his time in China but his letters to his mother give us a fascinating glimpse of a way of life which was soon to vanish for ever. He describes how the house has several brick buildings surrounding three courtyards, and says that the side of each building which opens on to a courtyard is made of paper and wood which makes the buildings very cold in winter. When you enter the house through the main door you turn left and then right and then left again down narrow corridors to prevent the spirits getting into the courtyard, as they can only move in straight lines (Harold was thinking of moving house, but discovered that the house he wanted to rent was already occupied by a spirit known as a fox fairy). The courtyards of Robert's house have a lot of flowers and shrubs in pots, and at the back of the second courtyard there is a tall screen to stop the spirits getting into the concubines' quarters. Robert was delighted by the flocks of tame pigeons which flew overhead at dawn and dusk with whistles attached to them, filling the air with wonderful sounds. The winter in Peking was bitterly cold with biting winds, but by April it was warm enough for him to go for walks in the parks and admire the weeping willows and the large tubs of black goldfish. He observes the approach of spring in his own courtyards – by mid February the camellia and the pot of white irises are flowering, and the orange and plum trees are blossoming. On Robert's birthday at the end of February the servants hang lanterns in the trees, but there is still snow on the ground. The tree peonies are out of their straw and have buds on at the beginning of April, and by mid April the main courtyard is covered in pink blossom. Just before Robert leaves for home in May the pots of nasturtiums and foxgloves begin to flower.

Robert began his homeward journey by heading for Japan, and had a week's holiday in a national park near Tokyo where he enjoyed walking in the countryside once more. From Japan he took a steamer to San Francisco and then flew to Washington to spend some time with his sister Lucy and her husband Ewan Butler, who was a correspondent for *The Times*. He returned to London in September, and after a few months he took a job at the Anglo-Iranian Oil Company. His task was basically that of a public relations officer, and he had to promote the interests of international oil companies. He was delighted to be given an entertainment allowance and to find that the Savoy Grill was conveniently located for hosting guests.

Once Robert had secured employment in London he was in need of a new cause to campaign for. Travel abroad was difficult by then because of the political situation, and so he started to divert his energy into preserving British architecture instead. He had always been interested in the buildings of his native country and back in 1934 had written *The Shell Guide To Wiltshire,* though not in the way that the editor of that series of county guides, his friend John Betjeman, would have liked. Initially Robert wanted to devote most of the guidebook to monologues on his own personal preferences of Stonehenge, Bradford-on-Avon Church, Malmesbury Abbey and Salisbury Cathedral, and when John asked him to include something on Georgian architecture he merely wrote that Wiltshire was comparatively poor in monuments of the eighteenth century. Eventually John lost patience and asked Edith Olivier to produce the gazetteer.

Back in London Robert was appalled when the Adelphi buildings, a terrace of 24 Adam houses by The Thames in London, were knocked down and replaced by office buildings. He was so enraged at the proposed demolition of Wren's All Hallows Church in Lombard Street that he wrote an article in the *Architectural Review* referring to the Church Commissioners as vandals. An idea to demolish all the buildings on the east side of Bedford Square upset him so much that he decided that he needed to take action himself to preserve London's architectural heritage. Together with Lord Derwent and the writer Douglas Goldring he founded a society which became known as the Georgian Group. It was initially a subgroup of the Society for the Protection of Ancient Buildings (SPAB). Lord Derwent was elected chairman of the Georgian Group, Robert was deputy chairman, and Douglas Goldring was made secretary. The Group soon had more than 100 members, including Robert's friends John Betjeman, Michael Rosse and James Lees-Milne. Lord Derwent was often away from London and so Robert had to chair most of the meetings, a job which kept him fully occupied in the evenings.

One of the first buildings that the Group tried to save was Norfolk House, which the Duke of Norfolk wanted to sell for development. They did not manage to save the building, but the Music Room was salvaged and put on display in the Victoria & Albert museum. The buildings in Mecklenburgh Square, however, were saved, and it is now Grade II listed. The Group successfully campaigned to save a pair of Palladian houses in Old Palace Yard, but had mixed success with its other ventures.

What with working full time and the activities of the Georgian Group you'd think Robert would have enough to occupy his mind, but he was also getting worried about the British Government's policy of appeasement. In March 1938, when German troops invaded Austria, he wrote to the *New Statesman* because he was so concerned about the low profile of the leaders of the Western European countries. He claimed that English civilisation and the freedom of the individual were in danger. He himself thought that it was now time for fighting rather than appeasement. He visited Berlin with his sister Lucy and her husband Ewan, a *Times* correspondent, to see for himself what Hitler was up to. Robert and Ewan were very worried by what they saw, and by September 1938 they had arranged for two million propaganda leaflets to be printed, ready to drop over Germany if necessary. Robert attended the Nazi Party Congress in Nuremberg with Unity Mitford and other members of the Mitford family, and the rallies, parades and congress sessions that he saw made him convinced that the West's policy of appeasement was wrong. He believed that Western civilisation was under threat, and wrote to the Ministry of Information about what he had seen. He did not believe that the Munich agreement meant 'peace in our time'.

In the Autumn of 1938 Robert went to the United States with the Petroleum Information Bureau and took the opportunity to sound out people's opinions on events in Germany and to assess American foreign policy. On his return to London he wrote to the Ministry of Information saying that if war broke out he did not think that the US would continue with its policy of isolationism. He thought that Britain should keep in the good books of the US in case it needed help in the event of war.

When World War Two started Robert tried to get a job with either the Foreign Office or the War Office but nobody wanted to employ him. His friends reckoned that it was because he was so outspoken. Instead he joined the European News department at the BBC, where he wrote propaganda bulletins. In December 1940, due to his knowledge of the Middle East and the petroleum industry, he managed to get a job in intelligence. His cover was Middle East War Correspondent for *The Sunday Times*, and in February 1941 he bordered a small merchant ship bound for Alexandria. Three days out from Liverpool the ship was torpedoed and Robert was killed. He was thirty five.

CHAPTER SEVEN – HAROLD ACTON

Sir Harold Acton (1904-94) was an Anglo-Florentine aesthete and man of letters who wrote poems, novels, and books on Italian art and history.

* * * * *

Harold Mario Mitchell Acton was born in Florence on 5th July 1904. He claimed that Sir John Acton, who was Prime Minister of Naples under Ferdinand IV, was his great great grandfather, but it seems more likely that Harold was descended from Sir John's younger brother Joseph. In 1829 Sir John's daughter Elizabeth had married into the Catholic Throckmorton family of Warwickshire, and as a keepsake of Naples Sir John commissioned a series of paintings of the city for her which can still be seen at the Throckmorton family home, Coughton Court.

Harold's family home, La Pietra, was one of many villas just outside Florence which were inhabited by members of the British or American ex-patriot community. Italy had a relaxed attitude to adultery and homosexuality, and when combined with the cheap cost of living it attracted a strange assortment of people. Writers who lived in Florentine villas for at least part of each year included Norman Douglas, Ronald Firbank, the Sitwells, Gertude Stein, Aldous Huxley, D H Lawrence and Edith Wharton. Norman Douglas, who wrote fiction and travel books, had had to leave London after a scandal involving an indecent assault, and Ronald Firbank who wrote fantasy novels which consisted mainly of dialogue was not averse to portraying social climbing and sexuality.

Harold recalled that when he was a child he had seen the eccentric Firbank parading round Florence with armfuls of lilies and distributing them to people in the street whether they wanted them or not. George Sitwell, father of the famous siblings, had purchased the huge Mediaeval castle of Montegufoni in 1910, and the family normally spent Autumn and Winter there. Gertrude Stein's brother the art critic and collector Leo Stein had moved to Florence from Paris because he disapproved of Gertrude's relationship with Alice B Toklas, but after a reconciliation Getrude often stayed with him at his Florentine villa. Aldous Huxley and D H Lawrence spent some of their winters in Florence, and the divorced New Yorker Edith Wharton was to be heard deprecating the accents of those Americans she considered to be from the 'Wild West'.

The Acton family's villa, La Pietra, had been purchased by Harold's father Arthur with money provided by his wife Hortense Mitchell, a wealthy heiress from Chicago. Hortense's father was the president of the Illinois Trust and Savings Bank, and Arthur had met Hortense when he was working in Chicago designing Italian-style palaces for rich American industrialists. He also designed a new building for his father-in-law's bank. Arthur and Hortense then proceeded to restore the gardens of La Pietra to their original Renaissance style, and to fill the house with antique furniture and old paintings. Many of the local villas were being sold off by Italians, and the couple took the opportunity to purchase some of their contents. They were particularly keen on early Italian pictures. Arthur also managed to make a lot of money by shipping art works overseas to wealthy American buyers.

The young Harold grew up surrounded by beautiful things, and this was to shape his interests and his outlook for the whole of his life. The Actons loved to entertain, and as well as meeting all those writers who were living in nearby villas Harold also became acquainted with Picasso, Henry Moore, Diaghilev and the latter's set and costume designer

Bakst. Many fancy dress balls were held at La Pietra. Guests often dressed in costumes based on those used by Diaghilev's Ballets Russes, and Harold and his younger brother William would be dressed as pages to match.

The Actons' nearest neighbour was the American art historian Bernard Berenson, and Harold would often visit him at I Tatti and admire his collections. From the age of about five Harold liked to tour the churches and art galleries of Florence, and he collected postcards of his favourite paintings. He also taught himself about non-Italian painters by studying his father's art catalogues, and was soon an expert on the French Impressionists, Spanish artists such as Velásquez and Goya, and English painters such as Constable. Family visits to Paris and the United States contributed to make Harold a sophisticated and cosmopolitan young man.

Initially Harold was educated by a Miss Penrose in Florence, who engendered in him a life-long love of poetry by making him read Shelley and encouraging him to write his own poems in the same style. At the age of ten he was sent to board at Wixenford Preparatory School near Wokingham, a feeder school for Eton. One of his fellow pupils was Kenneth Clark, who was later to remark that although some English prep schools might have been interested in educating their pupils, Wixenford wasn't one of them. Fellow students included Mark Ogilvie-Grant, Billy Clonmore, and Alfred and Hubert Duggan, who would all go on to study with Harold later at Eton or Oxford. Wixenford was where Harold met the sons of the English upper classes, with most of whom he turned out to have very little in common. His sophistication and his Italian looks made him stand out from the crowd, which is not something that small boys like to do. In order to avoid being bullied Harold decided to make a feature of his differences, and would tell funny stories to make the other boys laugh. In his spare time he wrote a lot of poems and did a lot of drawing, and during World War One he wrote an article for the school magazine stating that the quickest way for

Britain to win the war would be to wear uniforms designed by Bakst and commission Stravinsky to write battle marches. He was homesick for Florence, and he hated the grey skies, grey architecture and grey food of England.

In May 1918 Harold started at Eton College, where he met several boys who would later make their mark in the literary world. These included Eric Blair (George Orwell), Cyril Connolly, Anthony Powell, Alec Douglas-Home, and Ian Fleming. At Eton Harold championed Diaghilev and the Sitwells. He continued to write poetry, and published his first poems while he was still at school. One of his poems was printed in *The New Witness*, a magazine edited by G K Chesterton's brother Cecil, and some of his later verse appeared in *The Spectator*. As well as writing poetry Harold loved to read it, and his favourite poets included Edith Sitwell and Gertrude Stein. He spoke fluent French and enjoyed the verses of Verlaine and Rimbaud. The American ex-patriots Ezra Pound and T S Eliot also came to his attention.

Harold, an aesthete who was not interested in games, was lucky that Eton tolerated eccentricity more than most schools did. His particular friend at Eton was Brian Howard, who would become the model for Ambrose Silk in Evelyn Waugh's novel *Put Out More Flags*. Brian also lived for art and poetry, and the boys shared a further bond in that they both had American mothers. The pair had a passion for Diaghilev and avidly devoured reviews of his productions. Sometimes they danced to the music of Stravinsky and Rimsky-Korsakov in what they hoped was Ballets Russes style. Brian was jealous because Diaghilev had been to tea at La Pietra and Harold had seen the Ballets Russes several times in London. Fine Art was also appreciated by the boys, and while most pupils had prints of hunting scenes on their walls, Harold had a print of a Whistler nocturne.

In February 1922 Harold and Brian formed the Eton Society

of Arts, a club for pupils who liked music, painting and poetry. It was intended to be a discussion and exhibition group, and with their drawing master Sidney Evans as president and Brian as vice-president the Society met on Saturday evenings at Evans' studio. Other members of the Society included the future novelist Alan Powell, Henry Yorke (who would later write Modernist novels under the name Henry Green), and the future theatre designer Oliver Messel. Members of the Society took it in turns to present papers on different aspects of art, and topics which were discussed included Post-Impressionism, Oriental Art, Spanish Painting, and Colour as Applied to Decoration. Harold spoke in favour of the Post-Impressionists. There were also talks by external visitors including the president of the Royal College of Art Sir William Rothenstein, the artist and critic Roger Fry, and the art critic Arthur Clutton-Brock (father of one of the members of the Society). As far as Harold was concerned the piece de resistance was probably the visit by Edith Sitwell, who gave a talk entitled 'Modern Poetry' and also spoke about Stravinsky.

Harold and Brian were keen to have a vehicle in which they could showcase their own poetry, and they decided to found a new school magazine. In the end there was only one issue, but it sold out on the day of publication in March 1922. The magazine was called the *Eton Candle* (sporty pupils referred to it as the 'Eton Scandal') and sold for 2s 6d. That was an enormous sum for those days, but there were many rich parents who were willing to buy a copy. The magazine was dedicated to the poet Swinburne, and was a homage to Modernism. Most of the poems and articles were written by Harold and Brian themselves, though they solicited articles from old Etonians and also received contributions from Aldous Huxley and Edith Sitwell. Brian wrote an essay in praise of Modernism in which he stated that rhyme and metre weren't needed for true poetry and praised the work of Ezra Pound. The magazine also included a selection of Brian's own poems. Harold contributed a story about an aesthete who lives entirely for pleasure, an essay on Rimbaud, and 11 poems including one dedicated to Bakst. As a result of the publicity he received from the *Candle*, Harold's first volume of poetry, *Aquarium*, was published in 1923. The *Candle* also contained work by several other members of the society including paintings by both Harold's brother William and Alan Clutton-Brock. The magazine received a good review in the *Times Literary Supplement*, and *The Spectator* mentioned that it contained some interesting paintings.

* * * * *

Harold left Eton at Easter 1922, shortly after the publication of the *Candle*, and in October that year he arrived at Christ Church, Oxford. There he continued to write poetry and while he was still a student two volumes of his verses were published. In *Aquarium* he experiments with Modernism and uses strange words such as mephitic and nubirefousness. The poems show the influence of both T S Eliot and Edith Sitwell. Some of them demonstrate Harold's loathing of the industrial age in his descriptions of blast furnaces and factory towers, while others show his love of jazz and hot summer days. The second volume, *An Indian Ass*, received good reviews and led some critics to think that Harold was one of the leading poets of his generation. *Poetry* magazine loved Harold's unexpected turns of phrase and the sensitiveness of his poetry.

As well as writing poetry Harold also became an editor and critic. He edited a new magazine, *The Oxford Broom*, which was so called because it was supposed to sweep old traditions out of Oxford. Harold's new friend Evelyn Waugh designed the covers for each edition of the magazine and also contributed a story about the Lady Elizabeth who begged to be imprisoned with her lover Count Antony.

Writing in the student magazine *The Cherwell* Harold reviewed a book of poems by fellow student Graham Greene, saying that he found the poems both pathetic and sentimental. Greene, who found this criticism helpful, later made alterations to some of his other work as a result. Harold also wrote theatre reviews for *The Cherwell* which included some criticisms of the young John Gielgud who was based at the Oxford Playhouse at that time.

When he wasn't writing Harold spent a lot of time socialising. Brian Howard was still at Eton as he was having difficulty passing School Certificate and so Harold spent time with other friends from his Eton days including Robert Byron, Michael Rosse, Gavin Henderson, Bryan Guinness, Mark Ogilvie-Grant and David Talbot Rice. He also made some new friends including Evelyn Waugh, Graham Greene and Peter Quennell. The latter remembered Harold reciting Swinburne from memory at luncheon parties, and Harold would also declaim his own poems through a megaphone while standing on his balcony overlooking Christ Church meadow. Most of Harold's friends came from extremely wealthy families and did not need a degree as they would never have to work for a living. They entertained each other with extravagant luncheon parties in their rooms. Evelyn Waugh noted that Harold was the leader of their set and said that he was dazzled by his knowledge of the arts. He also found Harold very funny. Evelyn introduced Harold to a student drinking club known as The Hypocrites Club (it had the motto 'Water is Best') and Harold soon became one of the leading lights there. Evelyn and Harold, together with their friend Robert Byron, would try to outdo each other with their witty repartee and their outrageous clothes which flouted convention. Harold instigated the wearing of Oxford bags, and soon some of the other students were getting their own tailors to make trousers in the same style as Harold's. Harold had decorated his rooms with Victorian knick-knacks, which were by then deeply unfashionable, and Robert Byron vied with him to see who could have the best collection. They even tried to arrange an exhibition of Victoriana at the university, but it was vetoed by the authorities. By the time Harold left Oxford in 1926 he had done little work towards his degree (he ended up with a fourth) but he had begun to establish himself as a writer.

* * * * *

From 1926 until 1932 Harold flitted between London, Paris and Florence but wasn't drawn to settle in any of them permanently. During this period he produced two more volumes of poetry, two novels, and a book on the Medicis. The poems in *Five Saints and an Appendix* impressed the reviewers, who thought that Harold would go on to do great things. His next book of verse, *This Chaos*, was published by his friend Nancy Cunard and was only 31 pages long. This slim volume contains some poems on bizarre topics, including one where Harold is lying in his bath and talking to his sponge. Harold was unfortunate in the timing of the publication of his first novel, *Humdrum*, as it came out at the same time as Evelyn Waugh's *Decline and Fall* and was compared with it unfavourably by the critics. Cyril Connolly reviewed both of the novels together in the magazine *Horizon*, where he claimed that the satire in *Humdrum*, a novel in which two sisters end up swapping roles, was overdone. Another novel, *Cornelian*, was praised by Gertrude Stein but did not sell many copies. Both *Humdrum* and *Cornelian* were fantasy novels written in the style of Ronald Firbank.

In 1932 Harold's first non-fiction work, a book about the Medicis, was published. *The Last Medici* documents the causes of the disappearance of the family which made its mark on world art, literature and commerce, and deals mainly with the life and times of Cosimo III. Harold draws on contemporary accounts by visitors to Florence to give us a fascinating glimpse of the world of the Medicis. Bernard Berenson gave the book a good review, but it did not sell many copies.

During the 1920s Harold frequented the literary salons of London, including that of Emerald Cunard, and he mixed with all the writers, poets, artists and musicians of the day. In London he also kept up his friendships with the people from his Oxford days who partied with the Bright Young Things. When Harold's brother William left Oxford University their father procured a large house for them in Lancaster Gate. Here they were supposed to sell the old paintings and antique furniture which their father provided for them to display, but they preferred to use the house for partying. The house became one of the venues for the fancy dress parties of the Bright Young Things, but after one particularly uproarious party their father abruptly dismantled the house and William returned to Florence.

It was at the parties of the 1920s that Harold met Nancy Mitford. He had never visited Asthall or Swinbrook, but had heard a lot about Nancy while he was at Oxford from people such as Brian Howard. Brian thought that Nancy was wonderfully witty and that she was wasted on the Cotswolds. When Harold got to know Nancy better he became concerned for her welfare, feeling that she was wasting her time with Hamish Erskine. Nancy's marriage to Peter Rodd didn't improve things. Harold disliked Peter and considered him a conman, ultimately blaming the failure of the Rodds' marriage on Peter's inability to be faithful.

Another friend with whom Harold socialised in London was Evelyn Waugh, who dedicated his first novel, *Decline and Fall*, to Harold in gratitude for Harold's feedback on his earlier attempts at fiction. In May 1928 Harold acted as the best man at Evelyn's wedding. After the failure of the marriage there was a five-year cooling off in the friendship between Harold and Evelyn, which Harold attributed to the fact that once Evelyn had become a Catholic he didn't like to be reminded that he was divorced.

* * * * *

In 1932 Harold moved to Peking, where he found his spiritual home. He had been attracted to China after reading Arthur Waley's translations of some Chinese poems, and no doubt he also remembered his childhood love of the pictures in his copy of *The Emperor's Nightingale.* In Peking he studied Chinese with various tutors, eventually becoming fluent enough to teach English Literature and poetry at Peking National University. The image of Harold's students translating T S Eliot into Chinese is an amusing one. He also translated Chinese poems and plays from the vernacular, and learned to appreciate Chinese theatre. In 1936 the book *Modern Chinese Poetry*, with translations by Harold and his tutor Chen Shixiang, was published by Duckworth, and 1937 saw the publication of *Famous Chinese Plays*. Harold also tried his hand at translating short stories with the volume *Glue and Lacquer: Four Cautionary Tales.* His time in Peking also inspired a novel, *Peonies and Ponies,* in which Philip Flower falls in love with Yang, a beautiful Chinese boy. Yang is a living symbol of China and offers the prospect of hope to the ageing Englishman.

On the whole Harold avoided the ex-pat community in Peking and socialised mainly with the Chinese, including his tutors and pupils. He had himself painted in Chinese dress by Madame Lo Chang, one of the famous artists of the day. He collected antique Chinese works of art including furniture, bowls, vases and scrolls, and learnt to appreciate Chinese calligraphy. The Chinese way of life appealed greatly to

Harold, and he loved the patience, kindness and politeness of the people. He could happily have spent the rest of his life in Peking. However, he did not want to lose touch with old friends and corresponded regularly with Osbert Sitwell, Evelyn Waugh, Nancy Mitford and John Betjeman, giving them constructive comments on their writing.

In 1934 Desmond Parsons, the younger brother of Harold's friend Michael Rosse, moved to Peking and Harold found him a house to rent just two minutes' walk from his own place. Desmond was learning Chinese and he enjoyed going to the theatre with Harold, though he was disappointed that the Chinese actors didn't pay him any attention and refused to visit his home. When Robert Byron arrived in Peking to stay in Desmond's house after Desmond had left due to illness, Harold Acton took him under his wing and explained some of the Chinese customs to him. Robert couldn't understand why he had to take a rickshaw to Harold's house instead of walking for just two minutes, but Harold pointed out that Robert's rickshaw boy would be deeply offended if he went on foot.

Most of the Westerners who were living in Peking left in 1937 after the Japanese occupation but Harold himself stayed on, reluctant to leave his spiritual home and not wanting to return to his beloved La Pietra while Italy was in its current state of political upheaval. Some of his Chinese friends fled Peking but others chose to stay, and it was with them that he worked and socialised. He enjoyed discussing both English and Chinese poetry; to them the works of Wordsworth and Po Chu-i were equally important. Harold's main interest now, however, was the Chinese theatre, and he spent half of each day translating his favourite Chinese plays into English with the help of his old Chinese teacher, Mr Chou. He also went to a lot of performances at the theatre, where he enjoyed the intricate mixture of dance and drama. Unlike most of his Western friends he loved the high falsetto voices of the actors and the informal attitude of the audience who gossiped and drank tea while they watched.

Harold eventually decided that he had better leave Peking before world war broke out, and in June 1939 he headed for England via Japan, the Pacific and Canada. He was heartbroken at having to abandon his house and all his treasured Chinese works of art, but believed that he would be returning to Peking once the war was over. As it turned out he would never see his silk scrolls, lacquered tables or Ming-dynasty jade and horn cups again. In Japan Harold had three days in which to absorb a bit of Japanese culture before his ship sailed for Canada, but the limitations of his Japanese phrasebook meant that he was unable to converse with the inhabitants. He went to the theatre one afternoon and enjoyed the visual spectacle of the swirling dancers in their brocade costumes, but he was unable to follow the intricacies of the plot. He enjoyed visiting the temples and gardens in Kyoto, but found most Japanese buildings and parks looked toy-like in comparison with the open spaces he had been used to in China.

Midway on his voyage across the Pacific Harold stopped off at Honolulu and stayed for a few days at the home of his cousin Louise. She and her immediate family were away in London but Harold still enjoyed the hospitality of his relatives before moving on to Vancouver. From there he travelled by train and 'plane to Montreal, and arrived back in London after an interval of seven years.

* * * * *

In London Harold initially stayed with his brother William at his large studio in Tite Street, but as William was basically nocturnal the arrangement was not mutually satisfactory, and after a few weeks Harold moved out. William was going through one of his depressive phases and had more or less given up his portrait painting. He had developed an interest in the Indian sub-continent and was learning Urdu with his friend Beryl de Zoete, the companion of Harold's old friend Arthur Waley. Harold thought that William was homesick for Italy, and he was pleased when a visit by the Italians Tony Gandarillas and Marchesa Casati cheered him up. William and the marchesa shared a love of snakes (she kept a pet boa constrictor in a box) and when he was a child William had introduced snakes into the garden at La Pietra. In later years, when he was walking in the grounds there, Harold sometimes came across their descendants sunbathing.

Harold moved into a house in Eaton Terrace belonging to his friends the Michael Rosses' – Michael was away serving with the Irish Guards and Anne and the children were in Yorkshire. Harold was pleased to meet up with some of his old friends again, including Evelyn Waugh who had remarried and was living the life of a country squire, and the eccentric Robert Byron who was building an air-raid shelter in his garden. Patrick Kinross, John Sutro and Cecil Beaton often called at Eaton Terrace between air raids, and Brian Howard and Guy Burgess were to be found frequenting night clubs. But Harold wanted to do something useful to contribute to the war effort. He applied for a job at the Ministry of Information, but there was nothing doing. Visits to his old friend Emerald Cunard cheered him up, as she was both witty and kind. Both Emerald and Sibyl Colefax were still holding their salons, and at Emerald's he met up again with Gerald Berners, the Robert Abdys, and Diana Cooper.

In February 1940 Harold set off on a lecture tour of Italy on behalf of the British Council. He had been asked to promote Anglo-Italian relations, and the tour was an attempt to prevent hostilities between Britain and Italy. Harold desperately did not want his beloved Italy, the country of his birth, to declare war on Britain. The trip was to no avail. Harold's next job was teaching English to Free Polish airmen in Blackpool, then in

May 1941 he was accepted into the Royal Air Force as an intelligence officer and spent several months training. When Harold stood up on a training flight in order to get a better view, his knee was broken when the 'plane executed a steep turn. He was sent to convalescence for a while and then embarked on a refresher course in Chinese, hoping to be sent to Peking. But Harold's run of bad luck continued when the ship he was travelling on was torpedoed off the coast of Portugal and had to limp along. At Gibraltar Harold and his men were transferred to a Polish ship where he enjoyed the change of cuisine which included borscht. On investigating a complaint from the sergeants' mess, however, he discovered that the men were not so enamoured of the foreign fare as he was – they were very surprised when Harold said it was the type of food served in expensive London restaurants. What the men wanted was meat and two veg !

Harold eventually arrived at a barracks near Calcutta, where he was deployed on admin duties. He hoped to be sent on to China, but that was not to be. After several months he applied for a transfer, and was sent to Delhi as a press liaison officer. His run of bad luck continued. In Delhi he suffered frequent bouts of nausea and ended up having to have a kidney removed. In May 1943 Harold returned to London and was given a job at the Air Ministry. His old friend the Chinese scholar Arthur Waley was working in the same building, and they often lunched together. Emerald Cunard had by now moved into a suite at The Dorchester, having returned from America after her split with Thomas Beecham, and Harold resumed his attendance at her salons. He also enjoyed meeting old acquaintances at The Savile Club, but if he met Peter Rodd Peter would beg him not to tell his wife Nancy that he was home on leave. Harold himself would visit Nancy at Heywood Hill's bookshop, where he found her chic and energetic despite the hardships of war, and he also met her at dinner parties such as those given by Alvilde Chaplin, the future wife of James Lees-Milne. In October 1944, after the liberation of Paris, Harold was sent to work at SHAEF in Versailles as a press liaison officer, where his job involved censoring what journalists wrote about the conferences. One of the journalists was George Orwell, whom Harold had known slightly at Eton as Eric Blair, and they often dined together. Harold's friend Duff Cooper had been appointed British Ambassador to Paris, and Harold enjoyed attending Diana Cooper's receptions at the Embassy where he met the poets, musicians and artists of the day. In Paris he also resumed his friendships with Gertrude Stein and Jean Cocteau. He became an advocate for the revival of French art and literature, though he didn't like the Surrealists but preferred Bonnard and Vuillard. On visiting the Picasso room at the Salon d'Automne he noted that the paintings were being guarded by police because students had tried to vandalise them. The pianist Misia Sert, who was a patron of the arts and had posed for several artists, told Harold that she had burst into tears because the exhibition was so unworthy of Picasso. When he saw her tears, one of the policemen told her that she was lucky she didn't have to spend all day there like he did. Harold learnt a new word at this time, Existentialism, and became interested in the writings of Sartre, Camus and de Beauvoir, though he also retained a soft spot for Catholic writers such as Claudel.

In August 1945 Harold was sent to Germany, still as a press liaison officer, and it was while he was there that he heard that his brother William had died while serving in Italy. Harold's parents were grief-stricken, and he now felt obliged to give up any idea of returning to live in Peking in order to support them in their old age. During the war they had managed to make their way from Italy to Switzerland, but afterwards they returned to Florence to live in their beloved La Pietra. Harold's father, Arthur, felt that life without his collection of art works (he had five other villas housing them as well as La Pietra) would not have been worth living.

Harold flirted with the idea of becoming an American businessman, but after a few months in the United States visiting various relatives he realised that he was totally unsuited to that life and returned to Florence to settle at La Pietra. He began restoring the house and grounds, which had sustained remarkably little damage during the war, and soon took up the life of a writer again.

In California Harold had met up with one of his former pupils from Peking, Chen Shixiang, and together they had embarked on a translation of *The Peach-Blossom Fan,* a long classical Chinese drama about the decline of the Ming dynasty. Their translation was eventually published in 1976. Also while in the United States Harold had written *Prince Isidore*, a fantasy novel set in Naples and based partly on a work by Dumas. *Prince Isidore* was published in London in 1950, and later dramatised for the BBC by Christopher Sykes. When Harold moved back to Florence Gertrude Stein persuaded him to write his memoirs, and *Memoirs of an Aesthete* was published in 1947. Harold spent part of the 1950s in Naples, carrying out research on the Bourbons. His literary output after the war consisted mainly of works on Italian history and art, but he also wrote novels and short stories.

Once Nancy Mitford and her friend Harold were settled in Paris and Florence respectively they began a life-long correspondence. Harold kept Nancy's letters, in which she gave him all the gossip from Paris with her own unique sense of humour. He heard a lot from Nancy about Violet Trefusis, whom he had known since her parents had purchased Villa L'Ombrellino in Florence in 1924. Violet's mother, Alice Keppel, was a glamorous hostess. In her turn Violet told him about Nancy's goings on in Paris. Harold tried to keep on good terms with both ladies, though he considered Violet to be an exhibitionist. In Paris from 1923 onwards Violet had been one of the many lovers of the sewing machine heiress

Winnaretta Singer, who was the Princesse de Polignac by marriage. Winnaretta had introduced Violet to many of the great literary and artistic figures of the day in Paris. Violet herself wrote novels in the style of Ronald Firbank in both English and French. Readers enjoyed her books, but they were not considered great works of literature by the critics. Nowadays Violet is mainly remembered because she features as a character in other people's books. Nancy Mitford wrote about her in *Love in a Cold Climate*, where she is portrayed as the 60 year old Lady Montdore, who is vulgar and rude. She also appears in Cyril Connolly's novel *The Rock Pool* as Gertrude, who is charming but mischievous. Harold himself wrote about Violet in a short story entitled 'Codicil Coda' which was published in his book of short stories *The Soul's Gymnasium* in 1952. This time she is seen as an old lady who keeps altering her will because her friends keep dying. She is also writing a sensational autobiography.

As well as keeping in touch by letter, Harold and Nancy also managed to meet up occasionally. When Harold visited Paris Nancy would give cocktail parties for him and invite their mutual friends to entertain him. She liked visiting Harold in Florence because she loved the warm climate. Staying with Harold in 1965 she described La Pietra as 'complete perfection'. She loved the large rooms and the luxury and all the art works. The food at La Pietra was wonderful and Nancy also enjoyed eating out and visiting other villas and gardens. Violet Trefusis was away from Florence at the time but had urged Harold to take Nancy to admire Villa L'Ombrellino. Nancy didn't want to go, much to Violet's annoyance. She considered it a terrible slight.

Harold and Nancy also sometimes met up in Venice, and during the summer of 1970 they both stayed with Anna Maria Cicogna. Nancy enjoyed meeting friends and going to the beach and dining out at friends' houses. Harold was shocked at the change in Nancy's appearance since he had last seen her. She was quite ill, very thin, and had difficulty walking. They wrote to each other frequently after this visit, but never met up again. Harold continued writing to Nancy and sending her light novels to read right up until her death in 1973. He thought that it was Nancy's obsession with Frederick The Great and the enormousness of the task in writing his biography that had kept Nancy going for so long. Frederick seemed to have acted as an analgesic. In 1975 Harold, knowing that Nancy had intended to write her memoirs, wrote a biography of her which was based mainly on the letters she had sent him over the years.

Nancy was not the only old friend with whom Harold maintained contact. He was delighted when, after the war, Osbert Sitwell returned to live in the Sitwell family villa, Montegufoni, in Florence. He enjoyed Osbert's witty conversation and also that of his sister Edith, who often came to stay. He was amused when Edith described D H Lawrence as the 'head of the Jaeger school of literature' indicating that it was because he was 'hot, soft and woolly'. Edith wrote in her bedroom in the mornings but socialised for the rest of the day. Harold considered that, as he put it, Edith and her brothers had rescued poetry from the village pub.

Evelyn Waugh sometimes came to stay with the Sitwells, and Harold also met up with Evelyn on other occasions. During the Spring of 1952 Evelyn and Harold toured Sicily and southern Italy together. Harold had been feeling run down and was cheered up by Evelyn's droll sense of humour and wry comments on what he saw. He agreed with the French playwright Sacha Guitry's comment that it took three people to make a joke work – the one telling the joke, the one who can see the joke, and the one who misses the point. The one who understands the joke has his enjoyment of it increased by the fact that the other listener is bewildered. Evelyn told the jokes and Harold was the person who understood them. One is reminded of the woman in *Vile*

Bodies who went to Italy and found that some of the places there were named after cinemas in England. Harold enjoyed Evelyn's idiosyncratic sense of humour and felt bored after he left, though he later admitted to Nancy that Evelyn's insistence on behaving like the quintessential Englishman abroad by pretending that he didn't understand Italian and sending food back in restaurants had embarrassed him on occasion.

Harold often visited Paris and London and met up with Evelyn and other old friends there. He also visited people at their homes in the countryside, and stayed with Nancy's sister Deborah at both Chatsworth in Derbyshire and Lismore in Ireland. On other trips abroad he stayed with relatives in the United States and gave lectures at Chicago University. In 1956 Harold attended Marie-Laure de Noailles' Mardi Gras ball in Paris where guests had to dress as an artist, writer or musician. As Harold had been lecturing on William Beckford he decided to go as Beckford, and was glad to conceal his baldness by wearing a wig. He dressed in a pale blue satin costume and was very pleased with his appearance. At the ball he met lots of old friends and acquaintances, including Poulenc dressed as Chabrier, Diana Cooper as Lady Blessington, Pamela Churchill as Queen Titania, and Violet Trefusis as Lady Hester Stanhope. In October 1962 Harold went to a concert at the Festival Hall in London to celebrate Edith Sitwell's 75th birthday. Edith read some of her latest poems from her wheelchair. Peter Pears also sang some of her poems, which had been set to music by Benjamin Britten. Sir William Walton's Façade was played, with Irene Worth and Sebastian Shaw declaiming Edith's poems.

* * * * *

But socialising was not the only way in which Harold's time was spent during the post-war years. During the 1950s he spent a lot of time in Naples researching the history of the Bourbons and this resulted in two books, *The Bourbons of Naples* (published in 1956) and a sequel *The Last Bourbons of Naples* (published in 1961). Many long days were spent in the libraries and archives of Naples, and Harold also read a lot of private letters and diaries. The *Bourbons of Naples* deals with the period from 1734-1825 and covers the discovery of Pompei and the war with the French. Harold's alleged ancestor Sir John Acton features in the book, as do Napoleon and Nelson. The use of eye-witness accounts gives us a vivid picture of the Neapolitan court and way of life. *The Last Bourbons of Naples* covers the period 1825-1861 and deals with people and events during a period of great upheaval in Europe. The book is an important source of material on the history of Naples. Both books were well received by the critics, and Harold was pleased to be credited as a serious writer at last.

Harold also produced two coffee-table books about Florence. *Florence* (published in 1961) consists of 138 photographs taken by the Swiss photographer Martin Hurlimann, with accompanying historical notes written by Harold. *Great Houses of Italy: The Tuscan Villas* (published in 1973) deals with the history of the houses and the people who lived there, and has photographs of the exteriors taken by the German photographer Alexander Zielcke.

In 1965 Harold published his last novel, *Old Lamps for New. Tit for Tat and Other Tales,* a book of short stories, was published in 1972. *Old Lamps for New* is a satirical novel about a stolen picture, and is set in the contemporary art world where people are forging Vermeers and El Grecos. One art dealer discovers a long-lost Tintoretto, and another discovers that a painting hanging in a major London gallery is a forgery. *Tit for Tat and Other Tales* includes a story called 'The Machine is Broken Down' about the party scene in 1920s London, and one called 'The Gift Horse' which was later included in a book of short stories by contemporary writers.

* * * * *

After Harold's parents died he continued their tradition of providing lavish hospitality. American relatives sometimes came to stay, including his favourite cousin Louise who was not afraid to speak her mind. When Harold introduced her to the then Director of the British Institute in Florence, Francis Toye, who had written a book about Verdi, Francis told Louise that he had discovered Verdi. Louise promptly remarked that it was very odd that she'd been listening to Verdi all her life but she'd never heard of Francis. Harold enjoyed Louise's company because, as he put it, 'she warmed both hands before the fire of life'.

Other guests who stayed at La Pietra included several members of the British Royal Family including Harold's favourite, Princess Margaret. Harold had got to know the Princess through his friendship with Michael Rosse, who was the step-father of Anthony Armstrong Jones (Lord Snowdon). Prince Charles and Princess Diana also spent a week at La Pietra.

Harold continued to socialise with Bernard Berenson, the neighbouring American art historian who collected Italian primitives and Chinese and Islamic art. Harold was interested in the contrast between Berenson and Somerset Maugham, whom he sometimes met at Berenson's home, I Tatti. He had known Maugham before the war, when he had often visited La Pietra to play bridge. Harold noted that both Berenson and Maugham were elderly and that both were concerned about what legacy they would leave when they died. Maugham didn't care about what would happen to his French villa and his art collection when he died because he knew that he would live on in his writing. Berenson, on the other hand, wanted to preserve his library and art collection at I Tatti for future generations of students from Harvard. When he died in 1959,

Harvard did indeed take possession of I Tatti.

* * * * *

In 1974 Harold was knighted for his contribution to Anglo-Italian life, in particular for allowing the British Institutes's library to be housed at a property he owned in central Florence, and in 1986 he was made an honorary citizen of Florence. The Harold Acton Library still exists at the British Institute in Florence. It now has over 50,000 books, mainly in English, covering History of Art, English and Italian Literature, History, Travel and Music.

In his old age Harold was the centre of the small remaining British colony in Florence, and British and American journalists would come to interview him about his Oxford days. They found him charming and good humoured, and he was able to confirm to them that many of the events described in *Brideshead Revisited* had actually taken place. He enjoyed showing his guests round the garden and telling them about the history of it. The garden was open to the public on two days a week, as Harold wondered what he had done to deserve such beauty and wanted to share it with others. In 1978 an Italian movie featuring Nastassja Kinski, Cosi Come Sei, was filmed in and around Florence, and Harold allowed pictures of the garden to be used in the opening title sequence. When Harold died in February 1994 he was buried at the Cimetero Evangelico degli Allori in Florence. He gave his beloved La Pietra to New York University.

CHAPTER EIGHT – LORD BERNERS

Lord Berners (1883-1950) was an eccentric composer, painter and author who had a great love of practical jokes.

* * * * *

Gerald Tyrwhitt (later Lord Berners) was born on September 18th 1883. He was an only child who spent his early years at his grandparents' large home, Apley Hall in Shropshire, which had been remodelled in the Gothic Revival style. The Hall is believed by many to be the model for P G Wodehouse's Blandings Castle. Several of Gerald's unmarried adult relatives also lived in the house. His father Hugh was one of twelve children and so had no prospect of inheriting any money. At the age of 13 Hugh joined the navy, where he gradually worked his way up. He was away at sea for long periods during Gerald's childhood. Gerald's mother Julia came from a local wealthy family. Her main interest was foxhunting, though she painted in watercolours and sometimes took Gerald to visit the National Gallery and Royal Academy. Gerald also took up painting and did a sunset in the style of Turner, though when he showed the picture to his father it was mistaken for a painting of poached eggs and tomato soup.

When Gerald was six he and his parents moved to a smaller house in the countryside near Wrexham, where he enjoyed rambling and birdwatching. He preferred his own company to that of the neighbouring children, but enjoyed socialising with grown-ups. When two ladies showed him their sketches of Italy and Switzerland it made him long to be an artist and travel abroad. He wanted to escape from his routine existence, and when a visitor to the house played Chopin on the piano he was enthralled and begged to be allowed to have piano lessons. Music was his escape from reality, and by the age of ten he was already composing. His formal education began when a tutor instructed him in Latin, Greek and Arithmetic for two years. The tutor was briefly followed by a Swiss governess whom Gerald detested, and one of his earliest practical jokes was to blow up the outside lavatory when she was inside it. After that he was sent to board at Cheam School, a preparatory school in Hampshire.

At Cheam Gerald hated the food and hated games lessons. His only solace was music. He was allowed to continue playing the piano, and played in at least one concert. He also carried on composing, and in his final year one of his pieces was performed at the school concert. Gerald didn't shine academically but he enjoyed reading the works of people such as Dickens and Trollope and he also wrote poetry. His taste in painting now included the works of Raphael and Lord Leighton as well as Turner. With the help of some extra coaching Gerald passed the entrance examination for Eton College, and in 1897 he was fortunate in being placed in A A Somerville's house, Coleridge, where prowess at games was not considered necessary. Gerald enjoyed his years at Eton, where he spent a lot of time walking and swimming. His interest in art and music continued, and he liked sketching outdoor scenes. He discovered the music of Wagner, which inspired him to write his own opera. He wrote a light operetta in the style of Gilbert & Sullivan, where the owls went 'Tyrwhitt, Tyrwhitt'.

At the age of 16 Gerald was removed from Eton because he wasn't well. He may have been suffering from rheumatic fever. His father thought that it was time that Gerald started earning his living and suggested a career in the diplomatic service, so in 1900 Gerald was sent abroad to learn the necessary languages. He went first as a paying guest to a house in Normandy, where he loved sketching in the countryside. He also enjoyed the delicious French food, and found time to continue with his piano playing. The hostess's library afforded many books for him to read. To learn German he was sent to Dresden, again as a paying guest. There he enjoyed weekly visits to the opera, and also took lessons in orchestration.

For the next seven years Gerald travelled round Europe, funded by his mother. He spent time in Germany, France, Italy and England in order to prepare for the diplomatic service examinations. As well as studying languages he had to learn the history and geography of the various countries. During this time he continued sketching and he also made designs for cushion covers and screens, which he sent home to his mother. He still played the piano, and tried his hand at composing. He enjoyed visiting the theatre wherever he happened to be, and discovered the operas of Mozart and Strauss. Gerald's father died in 1907, and a year later his mother married again.

After Gerald had failed his examinations twice he was made an honorary attaché at the British Embassy in Constantinople. As there were no clerical staff at embassies in those days, and Gerald was at the bottom of the hierarchy, it fell to him to do the admin work. To add insult to injury, honorary posts were unpaid and designed for people with private means. In 1910 Harold Nicolson joined Gerald at the Embassy. They became firm friends, and in later years Harold often visited Gerald at Faringdon. A few weeks after Harold arrived in Constantinople Gerald was posted to the embassy in Rome. The ambassador at that time was Sir Rennell Rodd, the father of the Peter Rodd who would go on to marry Nancy Mitford (in later years Gerald and Nancy would exchange anecdotes about Peter). Gerald fell in love with Rome and got to know some members of Italian society including the Marchesa Casati who had monkeys in her drawing room, snakes in her hall, and hosted exotic parties. Sometimes the parties were a trifle too exotic, such as the one where some of her servants almost came to a sticky end after she dressed them as Nubian slaves and dipped them in gold paint. Lady

Rodd also gave spectacular parties and fancy dress balls which were attended by Gerald.

While he was in Rome Gerald continued to indulge his passion for art and music. He was still active with his sketchbook, and he also enjoyed going to hear string quartets. In 1911 he met Stravinsky, who was writing music for Diaghilev's ballets, and they became life-long friends. Gerald had almost certainly already seen the Ballets Russes in London. In 1913 Gerald composed *Three Songs in the German Manner* and the following year he wrote *La Poisson d'Or,* a piano work which he dedicated to Stravinsky. He was still in Rome when World War One broke out, and continued there as a diplomat throughout the war. In those days diplomats were expected to carry on being diplomats, and there was no expectation that they would become combatants. Gerald was never in any danger during the war, and he suffered only minor discomforts. He continued to socialise as normal, mixing with musical and artistic friends including Diaghilev, Bakst, Picasso and Cocteau.

Throughout the war Gerald continued to compose. In 1914 he wrote a second piano piece, *Trois Petites Marches Funebres*, which consisted of an official funeral on a rainy day, a child grieving for a pet canary, and a funeral for a dead aunt. This was followed by his first orchestral work, which was entitled simply *Trois Morceaux*. He was not interested in whether or not the public liked his work, he was just trying to define his style as a composer. March 1917 saw the first professional performance of any of Gerald's works, with *Trois Petites Marches Funebres* being played in Rome. During his time in Rome Gerald also produced two more works for the piano, *Fragments Psychologiques* and *Valses Bourgeoises*. The waltzes were first performed at the Salzburg Festival in 1923.

* * * * *

In 1918 Gerald inherited the title 'Lord Berners' from an uncle. A condition of the inheritance was that he take the surname Wilson, and so his last name became Tyrwhitt-Wilson. With the title came several large houses and a lot of land, and Gerald became very rich after selling most of these. He kept Faringdon House in Oxfordshire and the income from its estate, and installed his mother and her second husband in the house. He himself kept a small, bachelor flat there. In June 1919 he left Rome and moved to England. Not long afterwards he bought a large apartment in Rome, and thenceforward he commuted between his three homes in London, Faringdon and Rome. He also sometimes stayed at hotels in Paris. In order to facilitate his travels Gerald bought himself a Rolls Royce and had a small clavichord made to fit inside it. The clavichord was stored under the passenger seat in the place normally reserved for the tool kit, and if Gerald felt the urge to compose while he was driving along he would ask the chauffeur to stop the car and set up the instrument. He never learnt to compose without the use of a keyboard.

In London Gerald dined with old pals such as Diaghilev, the Duff Coopers, Wyndham Lewis and Osbert Sitwell. Through the Sitwells he met various members of the Bloomsbury Group, though he found them too serious for his liking. He also made new friends including Emerald Cunard, with whom he enjoyed going to the opera. At the salons of Emerald and her rival hostess Sibyl Colefax he mixed with many of the literary and artistic people of the day, famously describing Sibyl's gatherings as a party of lunatics presided over by an efficient nurse, and Emerald's gatherings as a party of lunatics presided over by a lunatic. Gerald loved to tease Sibyl, who was a social climber, and on one occasion he lured her to dinner by telling her that the 'P of W' would be there. She was most disconcerted when she arrived to find that the Provost of Worcester was dining with Gerald. At Faringdon he entertained some of the friends he had made while living abroad. His mother, who was not keen on foreigners, made an exception for the Marchesa Casati when she came to stay and brought her pet boa constrictor in a box. Her enthusiasm for the snake cooled, however, after it was let loose in her bedroom.

Throughout the 1920s Gerald continued to compose, and in 1923 he wrote his only opera, *Le Carosse Du St Sacrement*, which was produced in Paris in 1924 and based on a play by Mérimée which he had seen in Paris. He left the text in the original French, but cut some of it. The story is set in Peru and concerns a viceroy who is too ill with gout to attend a church festival and sends his mistress to the festival instead, lending her his carriage. On the way she gets involved in several accidents but is redeemed when she gives the carriage to the church and makes a friend of the bishop.

In 1924 Gerald wrote his final orchestral work, *Fugue in C Minor*. After this he turned his attention to ballet, and in 1926 he wrote the score for *The Triumph of Neptune*, which was based on a short story by Sacheverell Sitwell. The hero of the tale, a sailor, sees Fairyland through a magic telescope and decides to explore it with his friend, who is a journalist. The heroes get shipwrecked but are rescued by a god, and after traversing a grotto where they meet some evil giants the journalist is sawn in half at an ogre's castle. At the end of the ballet the sailor is turned into a fairy prince and marries Neptune's daughter. The ballet, which was written for the Ballets Russes, was choreographed by Balanchine and performed at the Lyceum in 1926. The performance was a great success and there were many curtain calls.

Gerald's second ballet, *Luna Park*, was a fantasy in one act and was also choreographed by Balanchine. It was written for C B Cochran's 1930 revue, and first performed at the London Pavilion in March of that year. The setting is a pretend freak show with characters such as a three-legged juggler and a one-legged ballerina. After a performance the freaks reveal themselves to be normal human beings and escape into the wide world.

* * * * *

During the 1930s Gerald did a lot of painting, and he produced many landscapes of the countryside around Rome. Corot had painted many of the same places, and on the whole Gerald imitated his style. Gerald's own collection of Corots was second only to that of the Louvre. 1931 saw the first exhibition of Gerald's paintings, which was held at the Lefevre Gallery in London. The exhibition was well received by *The Times*, whose critic compared Gerald's pictures with those of Corot and found that the former's had a greater use of colour and design. Gerald also painted scenes of the English countryside, but these were less colourful due to the lack of light. He tried his hand at painting the portraits of some of his friends, though he did Diana Guinness and Penelope Betjeman from photographs.

In 1931 Gerald's mother and her second husband died. Gerald took over the occupancy of the whole of Faringdon House, where he entertained extensively, though he still spent several months of each year on the Continent. He liked to be amused, and anyone who did not make him laugh was described as a 'dry blanket'. Guests at Faringdon House were asked to sign the visitors book, and people who stayed there included Gladys Marlborough the commercial traveller, Robert Abdy the obelisk fancier, John Sutro the barrister-without-law, Bryan Guinness the farmer, Adrian Daintrey the cannibal, the Marchesa Casati the tempteuse de serpents, Mark Ogilvie-Grant the plumber, Pamela Mitford the shepherdess, and Evelyn Waugh the prospective eunuch (after returning safely from Abyssinia the following year he changed his status to 'intact'). Friends who lived in the vicinity of Faringdon, such as various Mitfords, the Betjemans, Cecil Beaton and Gavin Henderson (Lord Faringdon), would be invited to tea and would often ride over. Gerald was very fond of Penelope Betjeman's horse Moti, and allowed him into the drawing room when the humans were having tea. On one occasion Gerald painted a portrait of Moti standing in the room, and in typical Gerald fashion he had himself photographed while doing so.

Anyone who visited Gerald had to accept that they would have practical jokes played on them and that they would be ridiculed. There were various notices around the house, including 'mangling done here' on one of the doors, and a notice in a bathroom advising guests not to drink the bathwater because there was an unidentified corpse in the cistern. Visitors were also asked not to fire guns, blow bugles, or scream between the hours of midnight and 6 am. In place of the usual gong, people were summoned to dinner by the playing of a music box. But despite having a wide circle of friends Gerald was lonely, and in 1932 the twenty-year-old Robert Heber-Percy stepped in to fill the gap in Gerald's life.

Robert had been brought up on a large estate in Shropshire and loved the outdoor life including riding and hunting. He was not interested in music or literature, and seems an odd sort of person for Gerald to choose as a companion. Perhaps he had hidden charms. After leaving Stowe School Robert was briefly in the army, from which he was asked to resign. He then worked as a waiter in a Lyons Corner House but was sacked after spilling soup over a customer (he suffered terribly from clumsiness and was often told off by Gerald for breaking his cherished possessions). Subsequently he worked in a night club in London. Gerald didn't keep a diary and it is not clear how he met Robert, though it may have been when he was a customer in the Lyons Corner House. A second possibility is that they met when they were both members of a country house party at Vaynol, the home of Michael Duff in North Wales. At any rate something clicked, and from 1933 Robert accompanied Gerald on his Continental travels, embarrassing his sombrely-dressed benefactor with his brightly-coloured clothes. During the months when the two of them resided at Faringdon Robert opted for the outdoor life and worked enthusiastically on the estate farm. He tried to develop an understanding of music and literature in the hope that he would be able to converse intelligently about them with Gerald's friends, but he soon lost interest and preferred to make himself scarce when such things were being discussed.

Robert seems to have had several affairs over the years, to which Gerald turned a blind eye. Gerald was just glad that his much younger friend didn't leave him. When the fabulously wealthy Peter Watson had a fling with Robert he gave him a car. Cecil Beaton was so jealous that he asked for a car too, and got one. In retaliation for the affair Gerald wrote a novel about lesbian affairs *The Girls of Radcliff Hall*, in which he himself features as the headmistress Miss Carfax. The title of the novel comes from the name of the lesbian author Radclyffe Hall, who had written *The Well of Loneliness* which was published in 1928. In Gerald's novel all of his acquaintances are portrayed as lesbian schoolgirls, with Cecily (Cecil Beaton) being jealous because Lizzie (Peter Watson) gives a car to Millie (Robert Heber-Percy). Lizzie likes living in London but Millie prefers the country, so Miss Carfax considers resigning and asking Millie to live in the country with her and keep chickens. When a new American girl, May (Peter Watson's lover Robin Thomas) arrives at the school Lizzie adores her as soon as she arrives and doesn't even bother going to watch Cecily acting in the school play. After having various adventures, Lizzie ends up as a nun. The novel was published privately under the name Adela Quebec, and when it came out Cecil Beaton was deeply offended and tried to collect all the copies and destroy them.

* * * * *

In 1935 the last folly to be built in England was erected on a hill at Faringdon. According to some accounts it was a birthday present from Gerald to Robert. The architect of the folly was Gerry Wellesley, later the 7th Duke of Wellington (John Betjeman said that he was the only modern architect with a style called after him – the Gerry-built style). Gerald was away in Italy while the folly was being built, and when he got back he was furious to find that a Classical tower had been built when he had wanted a Gothic one. The architect was made to add a viewing room in Gothic style to the top of the tower. The public were allowed to ascend the 150 steps to the top of the tower, though Gerald had a notice put up saying that anyone who committed suicide did so at their own risk. From time to time he liked to annoy the neighbours by spreading a rumour that he was going to top the tower with a revolving lighthouse and a fog horn. John Betjeman, who worked at the *Architectural Review* and was the general editor of the S*hell Guides*, used a painting which Gerald did of the folly for the front cover of the *Shell Guide to Berkshire* (Faringdon was in Berkshire until the 1974 boundary review), and for the cover of the *Shell Guide to Wiltshire* Gerald produced a collage of strangely juxtaposed photographs of country houses, pigs, local peasantry and elegantly-dressed ladies.

* * * * *

A largely accurate portrayal of Gerald's way of life during the 1930s can be found in his friend Nancy Mitford's semi-autobiographical novel *The Pursuit of Love*, where he features as the eccentric Lord Merlin who dyes his pigeons in pastel colours, puts necklaces round the necks of his pet dogs, has a folly on a hill near his house, and entertains a friend who keeps a pet boa constrictor in a box.

In real life Gerald did indeed have the fantail pigeons

at Faringdon dyed in pastel shades of pink, purple and blue so that they looked like confetti when they tumbled out of the sky. Friends believed that they were sometimes coloured to match the food which was going to be served for dinner, so that, for instance, they would be dyed pink when lobster was on the menu. Stravinsky's wife sent Gerald some blue powder with which to dye his mayonnaise, but he found it unappetising and Nancy Mitford, who tasted it, said it was disgusting. It is not known what Gerald's neighbours thought about the pastel pigeons, but when he apparently suggested that they should dye their cows and horses to match, they demurred. Gerald loved to tease his neighbours, and when he needed a telegraphic address for the Faringdon farm he chose the word 'Neighbourtease'. In *The Pursuit of Love* Lord Merlin's folly is even more of a neighbourtease than Gerald's: it is topped with a gold angel which blows a trumpet every evening at the hour of Lord Merlin's birth. Both Lord Merlin and Gerald have a friend who has a pet boa constrictor, but Lord Merlin goes one step further than Gerald. When he is visiting Linda in Paris he picks up a book of hers and reads out the words "Dieu, que le son du cor est triste au fonds des bois". This reminds him of the time a friend's pet boa constrictor got stuck inside a French horn. His friend rang him up and said "Dieu, que le son du boa est triste au fonds du cor".

The Mitford family were neighbours of Gerald, and Lord Redesdale tolerated him although they had nothing in common; Lord Redesdale was a typical landowner who liked hunting and shooting, and country sports were anathema to Gerald. Both Nancy and her sister Diana were very fond of Gerald and stayed with him in Rome and Faringdon on several occasions.

* * * * *

1936 was one of Gerald's busiest years. His first novel, *The Camel*, was published to favourable reviews from *The Times* and the *New Statesman*. It is dedicated to the Betjemans, and the Surrealist plot concerns a vicar and his wife (Penelope Betjeman reckoned they were modelled on John and herself) who find a camel on their doorstep. The vicar's wife, Antonia, takes to riding the camel and it becomes very attached to her; she ends up riding off into the sunset after a complicated scenario involving a murder and a suicide. There is also a gossipy verger called Beaton in the book (Cecil Beaton considered taking out a libel action because he thought his name was being taken in vain).

1936 was also the year of the International Surrealist Exhibition in London, at which Gerald's friend Salvador Dali gave a lecture. Gerald had first met Dali in Paris in 1932, and after they met again in Rome in 1935 they became firm friends. Gerald arranged the hire of a deep sea diver's suit for Dali to wear during the talk, and on being asked how deep Dali was going to dive he replied that he would be diving to the depth of his subconscious. Dali caused a sensation when he arrived on stage in the suit with two wolfhounds, a billiard cue and a jewelled dagger. The audience thought it was all part of the act when a workman with a spanner arrived to remove Dali's helmet, not realising that he was struggling to breathe and about to pass out.

Throughout the year Gerald had been liaising with Gertrude Stein to produce a ballet called *A Wedding Bouquet* which was based on her 1931 play *They Must Be Wedded To Their Wife* about a wedding in provincial France. The ballet was staged at Sadler's Wells in 1937, with choreography by Ashton and music, costumes and backdrops by Gerald himself. Gerald's final act of 1936 was to put an advertisement in *The Times* of 21st December offering two elephants and a small house-trained rhinoceros for sale, stating that they would make delightful Christmas presents. When Babar replied in the *Daily Sketch*, Gerald wrote back saying that he always respected people who were larger than he was, but the elephants had done a lot of damage in the grounds and then gone round the town ringing people's doorbells.

For his next ballet *Cupid and Psyche*, which had been under discussion for some time, Gerald produced some light music to accord with the choreography of Frederick Ashton and the sets and costumes designed by Francis Rose. Francis stayed with Gerald in London and they collaborated on the music and the set designs. The ballet was performed at Sadler's Wells in April 1939, and both *The Times* and the *Daily Telegraph* gave it favourable reviews. The audience, however, seem to have booed, and the ballet suffered from the perennial problem of how to make it clear to the audience that Cupid was invisible to Psyche.

In August 1939 Gerald was preparing to set off for his annual visit to Rome as normal, impervious to the coming threat of world war. When he realised that his way of life of flitting between England, Italy and France was no longer possible, and that people such as him who appreciated art and beauty were redundant in the modern world, he suffered a nervous breakdown. He shut his London house and went to live in Oxford, only visiting Faringdon at weekends. His friend Maurice Bowra found him a job cataloguing books in the Taylorian Institute. Robert had joined the army and was engaged in intelligence work in the Balkans and the Middle East, but returned to Faringdon in the summer of 1941 when he was invalided out of the army. He went back to working on the home farm and helping with jobs such as haymaking and driving the tractor. When Gerald had recovered a bit from his depression and returned to Faringdon his home provided a haven at weekends for friends who were living in London such as Nancy Mitford, Cyril Connolly and Peter Quennell. He became particularly close to Nancy Mitford, visiting her sometimes at Heywood Hill's bookshop in London. She was also a source of comfort to him when he suffered from delusions and had trouble with his eyes – at one stage he was wearing dark glasses because he was convinced that beggars were swarming round him because he had such kind eyes.

Gerald's visitors from both London and Oxford were pleasantly surprised to find that he still managed to serve gourmet cuisine at Faringdon during the war despite rationing; Billa Harrod remembered a tasty consommé made from Marmite and grated carrots. The estate farm provided fresh produce, and game was not rationed, though fare was more meagre during the week than at weekends. Friends also enjoyed the luxury of a warm house – even the corridors and bedrooms were heated, which was almost unheard of in country houses at that time. During the winter of 1941-2 an American Army hospital was billeted at Faringdon, and Gerald was delighted to find the staff willing to do things such as shovel snow and mend his radio.

In the spring of 1942 Robert surprised everyone by announcing his engagement to a lady called Jennifer Fry, and in July of that year they were married. Jennifer was the daughter of Geoffrey Fry, who had been private secretary to Stanley Baldwin and was a member of the Fry chocolate family. She was the niece of Evelyn Gardner, who had been briefly married to Evelyn Waugh, and after her marriage she moved into Faringdon House. Her daughter, Victoria, was born in February 1943, and Gerald amazed everyone, including himself, by doting on the baby. The marriage was not a happy one, however, and by the summer of 1944 Robert had had enough. He had all Jennifer's belongings put in a removal van and sent to her parents' house. Victoria and her nanny visited Faringdon from time to time, but in 1949 Jennifer married the poet and editor of the *London Magazine* Alan Ross.

* * * * *

Gerald had not been devoid of occupation during the war. In 1941 he was asked to compose his first cinema music, which was for a film called *The Halfway House*. The guests at a remote hotel in Wales called Halfway House each have a problem which is sorted out in just one day, with criminals being reformed and estranged lovers getting back together again. The somewhat creepy atmosphere is enhanced by the fact that the hotel owner's daughter casts no shadow (she was killed when the hotel was bombed the year before the guests visited). Later Gerald was asked to write a song and a polka for the film *Champagne Charlie*, which concerns the rivalry between two music halls. Several novels by Gerald were also published during the war. *Count Omega* is an amusing parody of the kind of composer whom Berners disliked. It has been described as a nightmarish fantasy, and may have been written when Gerald was in one of his depressive moods. In *Far from the Madding War* Gerald portrays himself as Lord Fitzcricket, who dabbles in various branches of art and realises that art is appreciated more when the perpetrator is somewhat eccentric. Lord Fitzcricket is described as fundamentally superficial. *Percy Wallingford and Mr Pidger* is a volume of two short stories. The first part of the action in *Percy Wallingford* takes place during a country house party in 1914. Percy is the owner of the country house and has suffered a nervous breakdown which caused him to resign from the diplomatic service. He has recently married. Later, when Percy and his wife are on holiday in France, she is asphyxiated in a hotel bedroom and people assume that Percy has murdered her because she was so boring. The eponymous *Mr Pidger* is a dog whom Gerald based on Wincey (Winston), the King Charles Spaniel belonging to his friend Teresa Jungman. The slightly ridiculous plot involves Mr Pidger's owner smuggling him into her uncle's house and being disinherited as a consequence. Gerald's last novel, *The Romance of a Nose*, has a heroine modelled on Daisy Fellowes, the wealthy niece of the Princesse de Polignac. In the novel she appears as

Cleopatra, who has a large nose and decides to fly to Thebes for plastic surgery. After her nose reduction she woos Caesar and defeats all her enemies.

During the war Gerald had let his home in Rome and sold his London house. When the war ended he was 62 and considered himself to be an old man. Osbert Sitwell found him rather sweet and pathetic. Robert, who went to an army reunion in London, returned with a new boyfriend, Hugh Cruddas, who came for a visit but stayed indefinitely. Hugh made himself useful round the house by arranging flowers and mixing cocktails, and eventually he took over the running of the establishment. What Gerald thought of this arrangement does not seem to be recorded. Robert was worried about Gerald's health and did not want him to lounge around doing nothing, so he arranged for a nice lady to come and teach Gerald knitting. She soon gave up.

When Gerald perked up he began to orchestrate a ballet, *Les Sirenes*, for Sadler's Wells. While he worked at the piano in the drawing room, Cecil Beaton was upstairs designing the costumes. The eventual production was extremely elaborate; there was a large yellow motor car containing Margot Fonteyn, an Eastern potentate carried by slaves was played by Frederick Ashton, and Robert Helpmann was an Australian opera singer who descended from a balloon. Gerald was in a nursing home while rehearsals were going on, but he managed to attend the first night of the production. From time to time he returned to the nursing home in Richmond when he felt the need for a rest. He kept in touch with old friends such as Edward James, Daisy Fellowes and Osbert Sitwell, and many including Nancy Mitford wrote to him regularly. Increasingly frail, he started work on a third volume of his autobiography (the first two had already been published) but never finished it. He died on April 19th 1950, and in his will he left Faringdon House to Robert.

Bibliography

Memoirs of an Aesthete by Harold Acton, Methuen, 1948

More Memoirs of an Aesthete by Harold Acton, Methuen, 1970

Nancy Mitford: A Memoir by Harold Acton, Hamish Hamilton, 1975

The Letters of Evelyn Waugh edited by Mark Amory, Weidenfeld & Nicolson, 1980

Lord Berners: The Last Eccentric by Mark Amory, Faber & Faber Ltd, 2008

James Lees-Milne: The Life by Michael Bloch, John Murray, 2009

Robert Byron: Letters Home edited by Lucy Butler, John Murray, 1991

Mad World: Evelyn Waugh and the Secrets of Brideshead by Paula Byrne, Harper Press, 2009

Europe in the Looking Glass by Robert Byron, George Routledge & Sons, 1926

The Station Athos: Treasures and Men by Robert Byron, Duckworth, 1928

The Byzantine Achievement by Robert Byron, George Routledge & Sons, 1929

An Essay on India by Robert Byron, George Routledge & Sons, 1931

First Russia, Then Tibet by Robert Byron, Macmillan & Co Ltd, 1933

Innocence & Design by Richard Waughburton (written jointly by Robert Byron and Christopher Sykes), Macmillan & Co Ltd, 1935

The Road to Oxiana by Robert Byron, Macmillan & Co Ltd, 1937

The Brideshead Generation: Evelyn Waugh and his Friends by Humphrey Carpenter, Weidenfeld & Nicolson, 1989

Queer Saint : The Cultured Life of Peter Watson who shook Twentieth-Century Art and shocked High Society by Adrian Clark and Jeremy Dronfied, John Blake, 2015

The Diaries of Evelyn Waugh edited by Michael Davie, Weidenfeld & Nicolson, 1976

Wait for Me : Memoirs of the Youngest Mitford Sister by Deborah Devonshire, John Murray, 2010

Lord Berners: Composer, Writer, Painter by Peter Dickinson, Boydell Press, 2008

Blindness by Henry Green, E. P. Dutton & Company, 1926

Pack My Bag by Henry Green, Hogarth Press, 1952

Children of the Sun by Martin Green, Basic Books, 1976

The House of Mitford by Jonathan Guinness, Hutchinson and Co Ltd, 1984

Nancy Mitford : A Biography by Selina Hastings, Hamish Hamilton, 1985

England's Thousand Best Houses by Simon Jenkins, Allen Lane, 2003

Robert Byron: A Biography by James Knox, John Murray, 2003

Brian Howard: Portrait of a Failure by Marie-Jaqueline Lancaster, Blond, 1968

Ancestral Voices : Diaries 1942-1943 by James Lees-Milne, Chatto & Windus, 1975

Prophesying Peace : Diaries 1944-1945 by James Lees-Milne, Chatto & Windus, 1977

Caves of Ice: Diaries 1946-1947 by James Lees-Milne, Chatto & Windus, 1983

Another Self by James Lees-Milne, Faber & Faber 1984

Midway on the Waves : Diaries 1948-1949 by James Lees-Milne, Faber & Faber, 1985

Beneath a Waning Moon: Diaries 1985-1987 by James Lees-Milne, John Murray, 2003

The Mitford Girls by Mary S. Lovell, Little, Brown & Company, 2001

John Betjeman Letters Volume One : 1926-1951 edited by Candida Lycett Green, Methuen, 1994

Highland Fling by Nancy Mitford, Thornton Butterworth, 1931

Christmas Pudding by Nancy Mitford, Thornton Butterworth, 1932

The Pursuit of Love by Nancy Mitford, Random House, 1946

Love in a Cold Climate by Nancy Mitford, Hamish Hamilton, 1949

Love from Nancy: The Letters of Nancy Mitford edited by Charlotte Mosley, Hodder & Stoughton, 1993

In Tearing Haste : Letters between Deborah Devonshire and Patrick Leigh Fermor edited by Charlotte Mosley, John Murray, 2008

Infants of the Spring by Anthony Powell, William Heinemann Ltd, 1976

Messengers of Day by Anthony Powell, William Heinemann Ltd, 1978

The Bonus of Laughter by Alan Pryce-Jones, Hamish Hamilton, 1987

Friends of Promise: Cyril Connolly and the World of Horizon by Michael Sheldon, Hamish Hamilton Ltd, 1989

Four Studies in Loyalty by Christopher Sykes, William Collins & Sons Co Ltd, 1946

L*ife in a Cold Climate: Nancy Mitford the Biography – a Portrait of a Contradictory Woman* by Laura Thompson, Headline Book Publishing, 2003

Romancing: The Life and Work of Henry Green by Jeremy Treglown, Faber and Faber, 2000

Decline and Fall by Evelyn Waugh, Chapman and Hall, 1928

Vile Bodies by Evelyn Waugh, Chapman & Hall, 1930

A Handful of Dust by Evelyn Waugh, Chapman & Hall, 1934

Scoop by Evelyn Waugh, Chapman & Hall, 1938

Put Out More Flags by Evelyn Waugh, Chapman & Hall, 1942

Brideshead Revisited by Evelyn Waugh, Chapman & Hall, 1945

A Little Learning: An Autobiography by Evelyn Waugh, Chapman & Hall, 1964

The Spirit of Place: Nine Neo-Romantic Artists and their Times by Malcolm Yorke, Palgrave Macmillan, 1989

Appendix

Who's Who

William Acton (1906-1945)
William Acton was the younger brother of Sir Harold Acton. William was educated at Eton and Christ Church, Oxford. Between the wars he partied with the Bright Young Things in London. He was an accomplished artist in both pencil and oils, and at his studio in Tite Street he painted many of the society beauties of the day. During World War Two he served in the Pioneer Corps and died in Italy in August 1945.

John Betjeman (1906-1984)
Sir John Betjeman was a poet, architectural historian and broadcaster. He was educated at Marlborough College and Magdalen College, Oxford. After university he worked for the *Evening Standard* and *Architectural Review*, and later edited the *Shell Guides*. He also wrote books on architecture and campaigned against the demolition of Victorian buildings. He is best remembered for his volumes of poetry, and in 1972 he was created Poet Laureate.

Kenneth Clark (1903-1983)
Sir Kenneth Clark was educated at Winchester College and Trinity College, Oxford. He was a museum director, art historian and broadcaster, and is best remembered for presenting the BBC Television series Civilisation in 1969. In 1933 he became the youngest ever director of the National Gallery, and from 1955-1960 he was chairman of the Arts Council of Great Britain.

Cyril Connolly (1903-1974)
Cyril Connolly was educated at Eton and Balliol College, Oxford. He was a critic and writer and is best remembered for

his editorship of the literary magazine *Horizon*. From 1952-1974 he was chief book reviewer for *The Sunday Times*.

Tom Driberg, Baron Bradwell of Bradwell (1905-1976)
Tom Driberg, who was educated at Lancing College and Christ Church, Oxford, was a British journalist and politician. He worked as a reporter on *The Daily Express* and for ten years he wrote the William Hickey gossip column. He also wrote several biographies, including those of Lord Beaverbrook and Guy Burgess. From 1942-1955 and from 1959-1974 he served as a Member of Parliament, rising to become a senior Labour politician.

Alfred Duggan (1903-1964)
Alfred Duggan, the stepson of Lord Curzon, was educated at Eton and Balliol College, Oxford. He was a historian, archaeologist and historical novelist. His works include books on the Crusades, the Romans and Thomas Becket.

Hubert Duggan (1904-1943)
Hubert was the younger brother of Alfred Duggan. He was educated at Eton and Christ Church, Oxford. After only one term at university he joined the Life Guards, later moving to the regular army. From 1931 until his death he was Conservative Member of Parliament for Acton. He died of tuberculosis in 1943.

Bryan Guinness, 2nd Lord Moyne (1905-1992)
Bryan Guinness, who was educated at Eton and Christ Church, Oxford, was an heir to the Guinness brewing fortune. After university he was one of the Bright Young Things in 1920s London. In 1929 he married Diana Mitford, with whom he had two sons. He was called to the bar in 1931. In 1933 Bryan and Diana divorced and Diana married the fascist leader Oswald Mosley. In 1936 Bryan married Elisabeth Nelson, with whom he had nine children.

Roy Harrod (1900-1978)
Sir Henry Roy Forbes Harrod was educated at Westminster School and New College, Oxford. In the 1920s he was a young tutor in history and economics at Christ Church, where he taught until 1967. He is best remembered for his biography of John Maynard Keynes. He was married to Wilhelmina (Billa) Cresswell, who acted as secretary to the Georgian Group before her marriage.

Brian Howard (1905-1958)
Brian Howard was educated at Eton and Christ Church, Oxford. He was a poet and writer who never fulfilled his early promise. Some of his poetry was published while he was still at Eton, but most of his adult writing consisted of reviews of poetry and novels. He was one of the leaders of the Bright Young Things in 1920s London. After World War Two he travelled round Europe becoming increasingly dependent on drugs and alcohol. In 1958 he committed suicide after the accidental death of his lover.

Gavin Henderson, 2nd Baron Faringdon (1902-1977)
Alexander Gavin Henderson was educated at Eton and Christ Church, Oxford. In the 1920s he was a prominent member of the Bright Young Things, but later joined the Labour Party and became a member of London County Council. He is famous for once absent-mindedly addressing the House of Lords as 'My dears'.

Hugh Lygon (1904-1936)
Hugh Lygon was educated at Eton and Pembroke College, Oxford. He was the second son of Earl Beauchamp. One of Hugh's friends at Eton was Evelyn Waugh, and Hugh is widely believed to be the model for Sebastian Flyte in Waugh's novel *Brideshead Revisited*. Most of the characters in the novel are based on members of the Lygon family. After

university Hugh tried various professions before becoming a racehorse trainer. He was killed in a motoring accident in Germany in 1936.

Oliver Messel (1904-1978)
Oliver Messel was educated at Eton and The Slade School of Fine Art. From the 1930s to the 1950s he was Britain's leading theatre designer of costumes and sets. In the 1950s the rise of kitchen sink dramas led to a lack of commissions for his type of work in the theatre, and he turned his attention to interior design. In 1966 he moved to the West Indies, where he designed and decorated villas for clients including Princess Margaret.

Anthony Powell (1905-2000)
Sir Anthony Powell was a reviewer and novelist who is best remembered today for his twelve-volume semi-autobiographical work *A Dance to the Music of Time*. He was educated at Eton and Balliol College, Oxford and worked for six years at a publishing firm before becoming a novelist and book reviewer.

Peter Quennell (1905-1993)
Sir Peter Quennell was a poet, biographer, historian and critic. He was educated at Berkhamsted Grammar School and Balliol College, Oxford. During his long career he wrote more than 60 books. From 1944-1951 he was editor of the *Cornhill Magazine*, and from 1951-1979 he edited *History Today*.

Michael Rosse (1906-1979)
Michael Parsons, the 6th Earl of Rosse, succeeded to the Irish peerage in 1918. He was educated at Eton College and Christ Church, Oxford, and was a friend of several of the members of the Eton Society of Arts. He did much work for the National Trust, and also served as Chancellor of the University of Dublin. He was married to Anne Messel, who

was Oliver Messel's sister.

John Sutro (1903-1985)
John Sutro was educated at Oxford University, where he befriended the former members of the Eton Society of Arts. At Oxford he founded the Railway Club and also funded the student newspaper *The Cherwell*. He went on to become a film producer.

Christopher Sykes (1907-1986)
Christopher Sykes was educated at Downside School and Christ Church, Oxford. After university he worked as a diplomat in Berlin and Teheran. He wrote several books, including a biography of Evelyn Waugh, and worked for the BBC as well as writing for several magazines.

David Talbot Rice (1903-1972)
David Talbot Rice was educated at Eton and Christ Church, Oxford. After university he worked as an archaeologist, later becoming an expert on Byzantine and Islamic Art about which he wrote several books. From 1934 until 1972 he was Professor of Fine Art at the University of Edinburgh.

Henry Yorke (Henry Green) (1905-1973)
Henry Yorke was an Englishman who wrote highly esteemed Modernist novels under the pseudonym Henry Green. He was educated at Eton and Magdalen College, Oxford. His first novel was published while he was still a student. After university he joined the family firm but continued to write in his spare time, and between 1939 and 1952 he produced eight novels. After 1952 he became increasingly deaf and reclusive, and did not publish anything further before his death in 1973.

Index

Abdy, Sir Robert 135, 151
Acton, Sir Harold 14, 17, 18, 19, 25-6, 40, 46, 82, 83, 84, 86, 88, 98, 105, 106-7, 111, 112, 118, 123-144
Acton, William 125, 127, 131, 134-5, 137
Another Self 36, 37, 39, 43, 46, 60
Architectural Review, The 39, 115, 116, 120
Ashton, Sir Frederick 156, 157, 160
Auden W H 68-9, 72, 75, 76, 77-8

Bacon, Francis 78
Bakst, Leon 124-5, 128, 148
Balanchine, George, 150
Balfour, Patrick 3, 40, 87, 111, 114, 135
Beaton, Cecil 13, 15, 19, 21, 27, 29, 47, 69, 70, 81, 135, 151, 153, 156, 160
Beauchamp, Earl 97, 107-8
Berenson, Bernard 125, 131, 143-4
Berners, Lord Gerald 15, 48, 95, 135, 145-160
Betjeman, Sir John 6, 38, 39, 45, 59, 75, 88, 93, 111, 115, 120, 133, 154, 156
Betjeman, Penelope 114-5, 151, 152, 156
Blandings Castle 145
Bowra, Maurice 33, 96, 157
Brideshead Revisited 15, 81, 82, 83, 90, 94, 96-8, 144
Burgess, Guy 36, 135
Byron, Robert 3, 4, 5, 6-7, 10-11, 12, 26, 27, 29-30, 31, 40, 45, 46, 64, 86, 88, 103-121, 129, 130, 133, 135

Capote, Truman 71
Casati, Marchesa Luise 135, 147, 150, 151
Chaplin, Alvilde see Lees-Milne, Alvilde
Charles, Prince 143
Chavchavadze, George 19, 40
Cherwell, The 82, 107, 109, 110, 129
Chetwode, Penelope see Betjeman, Penelope
Christmas Pudding 6, 29, 113
Churchill, Johnnie 40, 42
Churchill, Randolph 38, 95
Churchill, Sir Winston 9, 10, 49, 63

Cicogna, Anna Maria 19, 139
Clark, Sir Kenneth 77, 125
Clonmore, Cecil (Billy) 106, 108, 125
Clutton-Brock, Alan 128
Cochran C B 150
Cocteau, Jean 17, 54, 69, 70, 137, 148
Colefax, Lady Sibyl 13, 47, 55, 135, 149
Colquhoun, Robert 75, 78
Connolly, Cyril 14, 40, 57, 72, 74, 75-6, 77, 88, 93, 95, 96, 98, 100, 111, 126, 130, 139, 157
Cooper, Lady Diana 17, 22, 55, 135, 137, 141
Cooper, Sir Duff 17, 96, 137, 149
Country Life 50
Craxton, John 74,75
Cruddas, Hugh 160
Cunard, Lady Emerald 13, 55, 131, 135, 136, 149
Cunard, Victor 19

Daily Express, The 86, 87, 109, 115
Daily Mail, The 90, 109, 110
Daily Sketch, The 87, 157
Daily Telegraph, The 157
Daintrey, Adrian 151
Dali, Salvador 70, 72, 77, 78, 156

Dashwood, Helen 13, 47
Dashwood, Sir John 47
de Gaulle, President Charles 14
de Noailles, Charles 54, 70
de Noailles, Marie-Laure 17, 54, 70, 141
de Polignac, Princesse Winnie 54-5, 138-9
Decline and Fall 85, 86, 130
Devonshire, Deborah see Mitford, Deborah
Diaghilev, Serge 70, 124-5, 126, 148, 149
Douglas, Norman 123
Driberg, Tom 31, 86, 87
Duggan, Alfred 106, 108, 125
Duggan, Hubert 97, 125

Eliot, T S 75, 78, 126, 128, 132
Elmley, Lord 97, 107-8
Erskine, Hamish 3, 4-5, 18, 27, 31, 42, 68, 114, 131
Eton Society of Arts 26, 105, 126-7
Evening Standard, The London 85, 87

Faringdon, Lord Gavin see Gavin Henderson
Fellowes, Daisy 54, 159, 160

Firbank, Ronald 123-4, 130, 139
Fleming, Ian 68, 126
Fleming, Peter 93
Fonteyn, Margot 160
Fouts, Denham 71-2, 73
Fowler, Norman 79
Freud, Lucian 75, 78
Fry, Jennifer 158
Fry, Roger 127

Gardner, Evelyn 5-6, 86-8, 112, 158
Gathorne-Hardy, Anne 42-3
Gathorne-Hardy, Eddie 42
Georgian Group, The 45, 120
Gielgud, Sir John 129
Graham, Alastair 30-31, 85, 87
Green, Henry see Yorke, Henry
Greene, Graham 42, 75, 93, 129
Guardian, The 85
Guinness, Bryan 4, 5, 40, 45, 83, 86, 88, 110, 112, 129, 151
Guinness, Diana see Mitford, Diana

Handful of Dust, A 90
Harrod, Wilhelmina (Billa) 24, 158
Harrod, Sir Roy 39, 107
Harley L P 18

Henderson, Gavin 83, 106, 108, 115, 129, 151
Heber-Percy, Robert 48, 152-3, 157, 158, 160
Helpmann, Robert 160
Heygate, John 6, 88, 106, 112
Highland Fling 6, 29, 113
Hill, Derek 18
Hill, Heywood 13-14, 15, 43, 48, 95
Horizon 67, 75-6, 77, 98, 100, 130
Howard, Brian 3, 27, 40, 72, 98, 105, 126-7, 129, 131, 135
Huxley, Aldous 123-4, 127
Hypocrites Club, The 82-3, 107, 129

Institute of Contemporary Arts 67, 78-9
Isherwood, Christopher 68, 73, 75, 78
Isis 82

Jagger, Sir Mick 56
James, Edward 36, 160
Jekyll, Gertrude 50
Jones, Sir Roderick 43
Joyce, James 41
Jungman, Teresa 159

Keppel, Alice 17
Kinross, Lord Patrick see Balfour, Patrick

Koestler, Arthur 75

Lady, The 1, 6, 88
Lancaster, Osbert 38, 45, 64
Lawrence, D H 123-4, 140
Lees-Milne, Alvilde 23, 24, 54-5, 58, 61, 64, 136
Lees-Milne, James 3, 13, 14, 15, 35-65, 68, 120
Leigh-Fermor, Patrick 33, 34, 36
Lloyd, Lord 39, 43
Love in a Cold Climate 2, 16, 18, 19, 47, 139
Lutyens, Sir Edwin 50, 115
Lygon, Lady Dorothy 89-90, 97
Lygon, Hugh 83, 89, 97, 107-8
Lygon, Lady Mary 89-90, 97

Margaret, Princess 143
Maugham, W Somerset 19, 56, 143
Messel, Oliver 5, 20, 27, 69, 105, 127
Messel, Rudolph 105, 106
Mitford, Deborah 19, 34, 61, 63-4, 65, 101, 141
Mitford, Diana 4, 5, 28, 37, 40, 65, 86, 87, 88, 112, 151, 155
Mitford, Jessica 9-10
Mitford, Nancy 1-24, 27-9, 31, 32-4, 38-9, 47, 48, 61, 69, 75, 88, 95, 99, 101, 102, 112-4, 131, 133, 138-41, 147, 154-5, 157-8, 160

Mitford, Pamela 24, 151
Mitford, Tom 3, 4, 12, 36-7, 113
Mitford, Unity 9
Mortimer, Raymond 15, 21, 41, 96
Mosley, Diana see Mitford, Diana
Mosley, Sir Oswald 9

National Trust 43-4, 47, 48-50, 52-3, 58
New Statesman, The 99, 108, 109, 121
News Chronicle, The 9
Nicolson, Sir Harold 41, 43, 47, 49, 51, 56, 57, 58, 62, 147

Ogilvie-Grant, Mark 5, 6, 8, 12, 19, 20, 23, 25-34, 110, 125, 129, 151
Orwell, George 68, 75, 126, 137
Oxford Broom, The 83, 128

Palewski, Gaston 14-16, 22
Parsons, Desmond 36-7, 118, 133
Picasso, Pablo 69, 71, 73, 77, 78, 96, 124-5, 137, 148

68,
Pigeon Pie 11, 28
Plunket Greene, David 107
Plunket Greene, Richard 85, 97
Pope-Hennessy, James 41, 51, 57, 64
Pope-Hennessy, John 51
Poulenc, Francis 17, 70
Powell, Anthony 18, 68, 85, 88, 111, 126, 127
Pryce-Jones, Alan 37, 38, 42, 59, 68, 111
Pursuit of Love, The 2, 11, 15, 16, 154-5
Put Out More Flags 7, 94, 126

Quennell, Peter 24, 40, 59, 111, 129, 157

Railway Club, The 107
Redesdale, Lord David 1-2, 8, 27, 38, 113
Reitlinger, Gerald 29-30, 110, 118
Rennell, Lady see Rodd, Lady
Rennell, Lord see Rodd, Sir Peter
Road to Oxiana, The 117, 118
Rodd, Francis 11-12, 14
Rodd, Lady 16, 147-8
Rodd, Peter 7-12, 13, 14, 18, 147
Rodd, Sir Rennell 7, 147
Ross, Alan 158
Rosse, Anne 118, 135
Rosse, Michael 3, 4, 36, 45, 46, 115, 118, 120, 129, 133, 135, 143
Russell, Sir Bertrand 20, 75

Sackville-West, Eddy 41, 42, 47, 50, 57, 73
Sackville-West, Vita 41, 50, 56, 62, 64, 75
Scoop 90-1
Seafield, Nina 3, 5, 27
Shell Guides 59, 119-20, 154
Singer, Winnaretta see de Polignac, Princesse
Sitwell, Edith 75, 126, 127, 128, 140, 141
Sitwell, Osbert 14, 15, 96, 115, 133, 140, 149, 160
Sitwell, Sacheverell 57, 64, 150
Spectator, The 102, 126, 128
Spender, Stephen 21, 68-9, 72
Stein, Gertrude 54, 72, 123-4, 126, 130, 137, 138, 156
Stewart-Jones, Rick 45-6, 48
Stravinsky, Igor 126, 148
Stuart Hay, John 108, 110
Sunday Times, The 19, 20, 57, 121
Sutherland, Graham 19, 56,

28, 88, 89, 114, 131, 136, 63, 74, 75
Sutro, John 27, 40, 107, 109, 135, 151
Sykes, Christopher 100, 117, 138

Tablet, The 93, 95
Talbot Rice, David 29, 106, 110, 111, 129
Tatler, The 6, 109
Tchelitchew 70, 72
Thomas, Dylan 75, 78
Times, The 60, 108, 109, 117, 118, 121, 151, 157
Times Literary Supplement 37, 68, 128
Trefusis, Violet 16, 17-18, 23, 55, 138-9, 141

Vile Bodies 6, 86, 87, 88, 140-1
Vogue 6, 29, 69, 88

Waley, Arthur 132, 135, 136
Watson, Peter 3, 36, 67-80, 153
Waugh, Evelyn 5-6, 7, 15, 18, 20, 26, 30-31, 42, 76, 81-102, 107, 111, 112, 128, 129, 130, 131-2, 133, 135, 140-1, 151
Wellesley, Gerald 154
Weymouth, Henry 3
Wharton, Edith 49, 123-4

Wigs On The Green 8, 28
Wilson, Angus 76

Yorke, Henry 105, 109, 127

Notes

Printed in Great Britain
by Amazon